Guardians of the Gate

Spiritual Mentoring for Women

by

ANN PLATZ

HARRISON HOUSE PUBLISHERS
TULSA, OKLAHOMA

06 05 04 03   10 9 8 7 6 5 4 3 2

Guardians of the Gate—
Spiritual Mentoring for Women
ISBN 1-57794-455-0
Copyright © 2002 by Ann Platz
1266 West Paces Ferry Road, #521
Atlanta, Georgia 30327-2306

Published by Harrison House, Inc.
P.O. Box 35035
Tulsa, Oklahoma 74153

Disclaimer:

According to *Webster's Collegiate Dictionary, Tenth Edition,* the definition of the word *impart* is "to give, convey, or grant as from a store."[1] In this book, we have coined the term *impartation* to mean "that which is imparted from a rich storehouse of knowledge, revelation, and experience" (author's definition).

According to *Webster's Collegiate Dictionary, Tenth Edition,* a mentor is "a trusted counselor, guide, tutor, coach."[2] For our purposes in this book, we have chosen to use the term *mentoree* to indicate "one who receives counsel, guidance, instruction, and encouragement from a mentor" (author's definition).

Lovingly dedicated to

MARY WILDES CRUM

and

ELIZA PEEPLES MACLEMORE,

who have mentored me with so much
wisdom, knowledge, truth, and grace.

Contents

Acknowledgments and Impartations

I have always thought that Webster or someone equally profound should coin another phrase for "thank you." The words seem so small when the gratitude in my heart is so large!

I treasure the guidance of Trena Thomas, Harrison House's editorial director, for her passion for this project and her compassion on its author. To Bill Fowler and staff, I welcome the opportunity to join you in extending the kingdom of God through books that bring glory to the Author of all life. To you, Anne Severance, without whom this book would not have been written, my heartfelt appreciation.

Always, always at the top of my list is my family, whom I adore—you, John, my darling husband, and daughters, Courtney and Margo, who fill me with great joy and pardonable pride.

As for the women who contributed to this book, they enrich my spirit and bless my heart. To God be the glory for gracing me with the gift of their friendship. In return, I speak an impartation to each of them.

Pam, to you I impart a discovery of who you are—a recognition of the beautiful threads of your life woven through the tapestry of God's grace.

Eliza, to you I impart the ability, in your lifetime, to see how far your wings have spread and to bask in an awakening of each day's investment.

Martha, to you I impart a fuller comprehension of the power of your ministry—healing broken hearts, placing boundaries, setting captives free.

Charlotte, to you, dear friend, I impart a wealth of the true meaning of words and an ability to express truth beyond your own vast knowledge of the language.

Doris, you are a tall drink of water on a hot summer day. You refresh the souls of everyone you meet.

Mary, you are a life-giver. To you, I impart more life, energy, and time for reflection. Your presence is the essence of healing.

Pam, you are a daughter of my heart. Even though I did not give birth to you, you are as dear to me as my own flesh and blood. To you, I impart the inheritance of a daughter.

Linda, you are a mother's pride. I impart wholeness to you, my dear, and the knowledge that every moment of your life is in God's hands.

Jody, to you I impart the limitless love of God. May you see with your spiritual eyes and hear with your spiritual ears all that He has planned for you.

Jean, to you I impart the fullness of grace, the love of a mother, the caring of a sister, the blessing of my friendship.

Victoria, although you are not a mentoree, you are the redeemed of the Lord. To you, darling, I impart honor, grace, and all the blessings of a virtuous woman.

Suzanne, you are a part of my heart. To my Jewish daughter I impart the preciousness of who you are—bold, yet gentle; wise, yet joyfully childlike; a daughter who honors her mother.

Brenda, to you I impart the joy of the Lord and the wealth of wisdom that comes from acquiring an obedient heart.

Patty, to you I impart the true knowledge of your destiny and grace for your destination.

Lizanne, you are a deep well of the Word and of wisdom. To you, I impart the anointing of a spiritual feast and the ability to feed multitudes.

Introduction

Gates have always fascinated me. Ornate or rustic, majestic or run-of-the-mill, I enjoy the variety of styles used to safeguard the persons or possessions lying beyond them. While gates impose a barrier, they also beckon and entice passersby to enter and discover just what treasures and delights are on the other side.

To be opened, gates require a key, a password, or even a gate-keeper. Before we can wander at will among the enclosed rooms or grassy acres, we must first gain access. Within every woman's heart are priceless treasures, deposited there by God. These gifts, traits, and possibilities may lie dormant until someone opens the gate, recognizes the potential, and begins the process of polishing and perfecting. That someone is often a spiritual mentor, a trusted confidante with a view over the walls and into the secret garden of your spirit.

A mentor is sent for a season to preside over your spiritual pilgrimage. She offers the greatest gift one person can offer another—an objective view of you, sprinkled with insight, humor, wisdom, and love. Your mentor is usually older and wiser, a seasoned veteran of life, a warrior woman who knows God intimately and is willing and able to interpret His ways to you. Your relationship is a match made in heaven!

As a younger woman, I hungered for an older godly woman to mentor me—to encourage, uplift, advise, and correct me gently. She was sent. She arrived. Within the pages of this book, you will meet other powerful personal mentors who unlocked my spirit and stirred up the gifts within me, then stood guard as I began practicing the presence of God. Along with these contemporary mentors, you will also become reacquainted with many biblical heroines, women of faith who continue to mentor us through their stories recorded in the Word of God.

As I grew in godliness, I desired to take younger women under my spiritual wing and pass on what I had learned. Therefore, this book is written to younger and older women—to highlight and celebrate the coming together of the generations. I have attempted, too, to explain that unique relationship between women—a heart bond that always includes the Holy Spirit, who is the ultimate mentor.

Each chapter contains a key that unlocks some new insight, some gem of practical wisdom that will guide your steps as you journey along the pathway to a deeper walk with God. Step through the Entrance Gate of your inner life and learn how to recognize mentors as they are divinely dispatched to guide you; the Garden Gate, where you will discover your giftings and begin to grow and flourish; the Open Gate, through which you will move from mentoree to mentor and enjoy the privilege of training others; and finally the Kingdom Gate, opening to your own incredibly exciting future in the Lord.

He has so much for you! Are you ready? The adventure lies ahead. Come explore the infinite possibilities waiting just beyond the gates!

—Ann Platz

Part 1

THE ENTRANCE GATE
TO THE INNER YOU

They shall be ministers in

My sanctuary, as gatekeepers of the house

and ministers of the house....

And it shall be, whenever they enter the

gates of the inner court, that they shall put

on linen garments....

And they shall teach My people

the difference between the holy

and the unholy....

EZEKIEL 44:11,17,23 NKJV

Madame Jeanne Guyon

I have always felt an affinity with Jeanne Guyon, a seventeenth century Frenchwoman who passionately desired a life of prayer and spiritual intimacy and mentored others in pursuing the same path. Married to an invalid while still in her teens, Madame Guyon was left a wealthy widow not long after her marriage. Rather than prolonging her mourning or passing her time in idle distractions, as was customary of the noblewomen of her day, she sought a closer walk with God.

Her heart for the Lord is clearly seen in her writings in a book titled *Experiencing the Depths of Jesus Christ,* written primarily for uneducated peasants. Because of this book she was denounced as a heretic and imprisoned in the Bastille during the reign of Louis XIV.

Madame Guyon focused on helping others understand their need for someone to guide them in their spiritual journey. When she was viciously attacked for her successful ministry, she wrote:

> *They said that I was a sorceress, that it was by a magic power I attracted souls, that everything in me was diabolical; that if I did charities, it was because I coined, and put off false money, with many other gross accusations, equally false, groundless and absurd. It seemed to me that all our Lord made me do for souls would be in union with Jesus Christ. In this divine union my words had wonderful effect, even the formation of Jesus Christ in the souls of others.*[1]

My prayer is that this book, like Madame Guyon's, might endure for centuries, if the Lord tarries, to light the way for others to follow.

CHAPTER 1

One on One

When I was a child, I spoke and thought and
reasoned as a child...but when I became a [woman]
my thoughts grew far beyond those of my childhood.

1 CORINTHIANS 13:11 TLB

I grew up in a home filled with beauty, graciousness, and gentility, rooted in the affluent surroundings of the Old South, and nurtured in the well-padded, white-apron lap of Clara Profitt Evins. Clara was a rather ordinary-looking woman with an ample bosom, arms made just for holding children, and a perpetual smile on her dark face. I recall thinking that her eyes didn't quite seem to belong to the rest of her. They were wise eyes: warm, chocolate-brown eyes that melted into my young spirit and read the secrets of my heart. I lived in her arms and at her feet.

The family cook, Clara was also my other mother and first mentor. Until the day she died, only three months before my dear sister Mary Ashley went home to heaven, I loved Clara with all my heart. I recall following her around as a child, listening to her sage advice gleaned from experience—everything from the escapades of her rural childhood to the meaning behind the spiritual songs she sang as she shelled butter beans on the porch or rolled out pie crusts in the kitchen. Her culinary skills were legendary, but her wisdom and insight piqued my curiosity and caused me to hang on to every word she uttered. Many of her words were straight from God's heart to mine—including her people's Scripture songs that she sang to me.

Mary Ashley, our two brothers, and I were blessed with the best. Our home, "Willbrook," was a spacious farmhouse on our grandparents' plantation, due east of Orangeburg, South Carolina, where love and laughter were served up as generously as Clara's mouth-watering peach cobbler and famous fried chicken. The good-neighbor policy was still in effect in those days; and Mother, a gracious southern hostess, civic leader, and captivating storyteller, seized every opportunity to give a party and welcome the world inside.

Consequently, Willbrook was a gathering place for all sorts of fascinating people. I never knew who would be sitting in the living room next—the governor or a tenant farmer in need of counsel. Daddy, wise and loving, presided over the farm—his only other real passion outside of his family and law practice. He faithfully served in the state Senate for nearly half a century before his death in 1995. Safe in this cocoon, the four of us flourished much like the cotton crops of earlier years.

It was in the fields of nearby Norway, South Carolina, near my great-grandfather's farm, that Clara spent much of her girlhood. She often visited her Uncle Straker Profitt, my father's overseer, a tall, lanky man who was as reliable as a southern summer day is long. "Good folks," my father always said. Back then, you were either "good folks," or you came from "a sorry lot." The Profitts were "good folks": loyal, honest, faithful, hard-working people you could count on.

When Clara was in her thirties, she came to live at Willbrook. With no children of her own and a huge heart to match her girth, she nurtured all of us. She was God's gift to our family. For all of my young life—and long past—she was my guardian angel, a powerful presence who lived up to her name, a true prophetess who spoke into my heart deep things of the Spirit.

At a time when most southern women practically memorized Emily Post's *Book of Etiquette,* neither Clara nor I understood that we were engaged in another fine art—the art of mentoring—or that I was the student and she the teacher.

More Than a Mother

Grandmother Williams, a former teacher, corrected my grammar. Mother, charming and beautiful, taught me in matters of manners and proper decorum in the tradition of the Old South. Both women made sure the family attended church services every time the doors were open, while Grandmother's favorite pastime was to encourage us to memorize passages from the Bible. But it was Clara who planted in my fertile spirit a seed that would spring to life and flourish in the rich soil of our unlikely relationship.

Chuck Pierce once said, "God is raising up faith-filled, 'no-name' women who have the Word of God in their mouths—women who will speak the kind of wisdom that causes preplanned paths of destruction...to be turned around and redeemed."[1] Clara was one such "no-name" women.

A mother can be her daughter's best friend, of course, and can serve as her mentor in some areas of life; but a more objective party does spiritual mentoring best. If Mother or Grandmother Williams had dropped the same pearls of wisdom in my path, I might have been skeptical. After all, a mother is biased. Her tutelage is expected—even required. She can't possibly be objective. She may be anticipating great things for you because of her own unfulfilled dreams or because "this is just what women do in our family." Heaven forbid, she may have an ulterior motive! Mother/daughter relationships are often so close that they may be challenging and even painful at times.

When God brings a mentor into your life, He appoints and anoints her for the task. (1 Tim. 1:1, 2, 12, 18; Matt. 28:19, 20.) There will be no controlling spirit, no fear—only freedom to learn and grow. Her personality will mesh with yours. She will be able to see what others cannot. Under the guidance of the Holy Spirit, she can shed light for a lifetime. You will see yourself as you really are—with all your gifts and talents—and who you are meant to be. You will know with an inner knowing that what she is saying about you is true. Your mentor is a spiritual link with the Lord.

With only a fourth-grade education, Clara had it all. She knew how to listen and she knew when to speak. She and the Lord had an ongoing dialogue, and sometimes I was the recipient of some of the gems He handed her. A devout Christian, she faithfully attended her own church on Sundays, then lived out all week what she had learned. Her only vice was a penchant for smoking a pipe, leaving her with the faint aroma of cherry blend tobacco, but she never smoked in my presence. I trusted her with my life. Daddy and Mother did too.

Further, she seemed to know things about me that I didn't even know about myself. I wanted to find out who had told her. It was no wonder that I was her small shadow.

When the Heart Is Hungry

There is only so much we can learn on our own. We all need some wiser head, some seasoned veteran of life to show us the way. There will come a time when the Holy Spirit has plowed your inner fields and you are ready to receive. It may follow some life-shattering experience—a serious financial setback, a divorce, the death of a loved one—when there are more questions than answers.

You may have arrived at a spiritual plateau. You're going nowhere fast and need a boost to reach the next level. Or you may simply know that you don't know, and your heart is hungry for more. Whatever the circumstances surrounding your teachable moment, you are wide open to something new.

God has been waiting for this moment. "Ask me and I will tell you some remarkable secrets about what is going to happen," He invites us through the prophet Jeremiah (Jer. 33:3). "Ask, and you will be given what you ask for. Seek and you will find. Knock, and the door will be opened," promised Jesus, in His unforgettable Sermon on the Mount (Matt. 7:7). "Begin to search again for Jehovah your God, and you shall find him when you search for him with all your hearts and souls" (Deut. 4:29). Propelled by our desire to know our destiny in Him, we will soon learn how to recognize the helpers sent by God to lead us into His fullness and to some "remarkable secrets."

I have always been intrigued by "remarkable secrets." "Unsearchable things," says the *New King James Version*. My inquisitive mind has wondered why things happen the way they do. What's going to be next? How will it all turn out? In my childhood I was too young to know, and Clara was too wise to point out her obvious edge in both wisdom and longevity. Still, I sensed that she was someone special. I knew that if I stayed nearby, I was apt to pick up something wise and wonderful.

When I probed too deeply—about the issue of slavery, for example, which I heard of in much of her singing—she simply chuckled and sidestepped the question with a question of her own. "Lord, you think everything is your business?"

At that early age of five or six, I was like a sponge, soaking up everything I could learn. It was my business to learn, wasn't it? "Lotta things ain't right in this world," she would continue, "but only One can set it straight..." I held my breath, waiting for her to finish. "Your *daddy*," I was sure she would say, but it was *Jesus* she mentioned: "Jesus, who knew all about black folks's troubles. Jesus, who could make it all better."

Ever practical, I wanted to know *how* He was going to do *that*.

"Oh, He's got His ways. The Lord—He ain't in no hurry. He owns all the time there is." This she said with such satisfaction that her eyes would close and she would rock back in her chair, signaling an end to the conversation.

Clara was a deep well from which a constant stream of unconditional love and peace flowed. It felt so right in her lap—whether being rocked into dreamland or hearing her songs in the night. With wisdom and restraint, she tweaked my curiosity about life, death, and holiness, constantly painting a picture of invisible things. It was a little game we played, but my heart was hungry and thirsty and I would not be satisfied until I had tapped into the depths. Clara started my lifelong quest to know God and my place in His plan.

The Ultimate Mentor

Clara was a gift from God, though at that time I did not clearly understand His plan. I was a seeker but was not actively looking for a mentor. I was just doing what children do: growing up. I was enjoying my surroundings—the joy of family, my southern heritage, life on a busy farm. I was storing up rich memories, yet feeling something stirring deep inside that demanded completion. It was the Holy Spirit who knew I needed direction, even at this tender age. He sent Clara, but He was there first.

It took a whole movement before many people in the church recognized the third Person of the Trinity. Jesus knew Him from the beginning, before the foundations of the world. (Heb. 9:14.) The Spirit of God is eternal, coexisting with Father and Son. He liked to refer to the Holy Spirit as "the Helper," "the Spirit of Truth," "the Teacher," "the Comforter," "the Counselor." Although Jesus modeled mentoring in His life on earth, the Holy Spirit is also our ultimate Mentor.

The Spirit of God is a worthy role model—perfect holiness, spiritual maturity, and wisdom. He *is* the Spirit of Truth. He prays for us with "groanings which cannot be uttered" (Rom. 8:26 NKJV). He hears our prayers with a listening heart. He recognizes our potential and is aware of the work the Father has already begun in us. He is utterly trustworthy, yet He allows us plenty of space. He is the fullness of life we crave.

Sometimes, however, we need to see God "with skin on." That's when He supernaturally connects us with someone who can encourage and cheer us on.

Recently I received a phone call from a dear friend who shared an intimate experience with me. In a letter to her adopted daughter, she wrote that the child "was like a beautiful rose. The finest roses are the ones that have been grafted onto the strongest roots," she went on. This child was so special that God sent her to my friend to be grafted onto *her* root system, to receive all the love and support she had to give.

My friend wasn't aware of it, but she was describing the mentoring relationship.

The weaker, younger person—the mentoree—is grafted onto the older, wiser one—the mentor—in order to be nurtured for a season. The mentor, in turn, is rooted in the living God. He is the vine and we are the branches. (John 15:5.) When the bloom bursts forth in all of its beauty, it is not the result of a natural birth but of a spiritual one.

This divine connection can only take place when we listen to the Spirit's still, small voice. Those little nudgings and promptings can come in the midst of frantic activity, but more often when we take time to be quiet, to wait, to be led "beside the still waters" (Ps. 23:2 NKJV).

The Shepherdess

Because Willbrook is a crop plantation, my family never raised sheep, but I do know something about them. Sheep are useful, although notoriously stupid and completely helpless creatures. Sheep tend to be sociable. They cluster together and are easily led; but on the slightest whim one may wander away from the flock, requiring the shepherd (or shepherdess) to leave the others and retrieve the stray.

In moving water, woolly sheep are top-heavy and may lose their footing, quickly becoming waterlogged. They will drown if not quickly rescued. That's why the psalmist speaks of leading the sheep "beside *still* waters."

More often they are likely to fall into some crevice or become tangled up in a thorn bush. Again the shepherd must leave the many to bring back the lost one, using his staff, crooked at one end, to snag the animal and pull him to safety.

I have also been told that ancient shepherds of the Middle East would lie down across the entrance to the sheepfold at night, serving as the *gate,* so that none of his foolish charges could escape without his notice and stumble off into the darkness.

Attracted by the world's delights and pleasures and often ignorant of its dangers, we are just as prone to wander. We may fall for Satan's lies and focus on our own insecurities and weaknesses rather than our unique God-given virtues. If we are like sheep, mentors are like shepherds—or shepherdesses—who stand guard to make sure we do not wander away and plunge into some deep pit of sin.

In Provence, an area of France where sheep and shepherds are a popular theme, I have purchased fine toile fabrics for clients in my design business. In this pattern, the shepherdess is depicted as a lovely figure, dressed in pale pinks and blues or greens, and wearing a bonnet and gloves. With her staff in one hand, she watches over her flock.

This is a seasoned woman of wisdom who has learned from her own life experiences and is now ready to pass on the benefit of her years. God raises up such shepherdesses to mother His children. They are the Lord's women, mighty women of faith, who are commissioned to be reverent in the way they live and to teach what is good. (Titus 2:3.)

I have to chuckle a little when I consider God's sense of humor in first sending me Clara. She, too, was a shepherdess, tending her own little flock of four. With her wig slightly askew, her black-rimmed glasses perched on her nose, and her snowy white apron, she guarded us well. No intruder dared venture into our garden paradise—not even a black snake we encountered on the path one day. She quickly grabbed a garden tool and put an end to the unfortunate reptile. She was a shepherdess with a hoe!

Whenever Clara was near, I never worried about anything. Her strength and common-sense remedies for life's ills brought such peace and security, and she continued to be my fount of spiritual knowledge until the end of her life.

I recall the last time Clara and I were together. She must have been past eighty. After her stroke, I was visiting at her bedside, trying to accustom myself to the possibility that she might soon leave us. Every memory was precious. She had so instilled in me a love for the deeper things of the Spirit that I could not bear the thought of life without her endless resources: no pretense, no guile, no politics.

"Clara," I began at last, "tell me what you remember about me as a child."

"Oh, I remember it so well," she said, her dark eyes welling up with tears that trickled down her leathery cheeks. "You children would have your fusses now and then, but when your daddy wanted to know the real truth he sent for *you*."

Honesty is a foundational part of my character, and it had taken Clara to reveal that precious truth to me. I blinked back tears, too, recalling a Christmas after I was married when I had attempted to see past the no-nonsense facade to the sensitive woman within. My gift to her that year was baby-blue towels, monogrammed with her initials—towels much like the ones Mother had on display in one of our guest bathrooms at Willbrook.

I will never forget the look on Clara's face when she opened the package, parted the tissue, and saw what was inside. She looked at those towels and then at me—from one to the other—again and again. I could see that I had given her something so precious that the gift transcended language.

But when I hung them, layered like Mother's, in her own bathroom, she erupted into one of those deep belly laughs that has come to be associated with her. Clara might not look the part; but inside,

where it mattered, Clara was a lady—and a lady has monogrammed towels. Shepherded by this woman almost since birth, I was able to repay her, at least in part, for all the years of watching over me, guarding the gates of my young spirit.

Now That We've Met

Now that we've met and you know a little something about me, let me tell you how important I believe it is for you to look for your spiritual mentor: one who will help you access the path to all God's delights for you, one who will stand guard over the gates to the inner you as you discover true intimacy with Him. Allow me the privilege of serving as one of the women God has sent to escort you to His holy heart.

CHAPTER 2

Recognizing Your Gatekeepers

You should follow my example, just as I follow Christ's.

1 CORINTHIANS 11:1

Before we go deeper together, maybe it's only fair to tell you that I am a "steel magnolia." I may have been born in the South, but I am no shrinking violet, languishing in the shade all day and sipping iced tea. I have been equipped by the Lord to be strong and very courageous. (Josh. 1:9.) When I have a message of extreme urgency for you, I will speak boldly.

I am eager for you to hear His heart, so listen carefully: *True mentors are in partnership with the Holy Spirit.* Apart from Him, there is no learning, no growth, no development, no experiencing of holy things. Therefore, you will recognize your next mentor when she persistently points you to God, not insisting on commandeering your life as her next do-gooder project.

On a trip to England with some lifelong friends, I once toured the lush countryside with its great estates dating back many centuries. One was a fabulous manor house gracing 8000 acres of beautifully landscaped lawns and gardens.

A portion of the manor house itself was enclosed by high stone walls, secured by massive iron gates displaying the family coat of arms. Immediately my feminine intuition kicked in, and my friend and I exchanged a knowing look. Something very valuable surely lay behind that protective barrier, and we were eager to find out what it was! With all those green acres to explore, the only thing on our minds was seeing whatever was on the other side of those gates.

How were we to get in? The gates were closed and locked, and there seemed to be no gatekeeper in sight. To compound the problem, the pointed spikes at the top of the iron shafts would discourage even the most determined tourist. Only an Olympic pole-vaulter could hope to force an entry here!

Always the persuasive person, I was sure that if I could just find someone in authority, I could talk our way into this inner sanctum. Just at that moment, around the corner walked a sprightly little man dressed in work attire, a giant ring of keys dangling from a loop on his belt. When he bobbed his head in a friendly greeting, the feather in his hat waved jauntily. This was obviously the very person we were looking for. There were enough keys in his possession to unlock all the doors and gateways from here to London.

Though he appeared to be on his way to attend to some chore or other, he kindly took time to satisfy our curiosity. This was a private garden, he explained, where the lady of the manor came to enjoy the tranquility and solitude. This area was not open to the public.

We were disappointed, of course, but understood the family's need for privacy and contented ourselves with a few peeks through the relief in the stonework of the walls at glimpses of the enticing scene within. Oh well, we had several days left. Maybe the next gates would open to us.

While it is not always possible to recognize a potential mentor when you meet one, she will resemble the gatekeeper of the great English manor in the following ways.

She Walks in the Authority of the Word

Eager to get inside to see all the delights of that private enclosure, I looked for someone who was authorized to unlock the gate. The man who appeared was obviously intimately acquainted with the life and habits of the master of the estate. I gathered that this was a trusted employee who knew the family and their needs well—even the personal need of his mistress for moments of refreshing from the demands made upon her as lady of the manor.

When your mentor arrives, you will note a quality of authority that comes from knowing her Master well. She will be intimately acquainted with Him because she has spent much time in His presence, hearing His instructions and learning to obey. She has tuned her heart to His; and, knowing *Him,* she is filled with wisdom and revelation knowledge for *you.*

Let me hasten to add that *all* authority comes from God. "For there is no authority except from God, and the authorities that exist are appointed by God...for they are God's ministers" (Rom. 13:1,6 NKJV). Your mentor will have only the authority the Lord has entrusted to her. If she continually refers you to Scripture to confirm something she has said, you will know immediately that she is under submission to Him and is not speaking on her own.

The Bible is God's Word. We might even say it is God's *breath.* "All Scripture is given by inspiration of God" (2 Tim. 3:16 NKJV). The word *inspiration* comes from the Latin word *in spiro,* which means to "breathe in."¹ When you read His Word or hear your mentor read passages God has impressed upon her to share with you, you will feel the breath of God blowing across your spirit. It is something like receiving spiritual CPR as you inhale deeply of His Word, allowing the power of the Scriptures to transform you and fill you with new life.

She Is Sensitive to the Season

The gatekeeper of the English estate, engaged in fulfilling his master's orders, could have been too busy to answer our questions that day. He might have hurried by without so much as acknowledging our presence. But he was friendly and kind, seemingly understanding our need to know something more about this elusive garden and knowing that, as tourists, we had limited time there.

Your mentor, too, will instinctively understand your need to know. She will perceive your hunger and thirst for spiritual things and will never pass by without imparting some word of encouragement or wisdom.

She is acting on orders from the Master, who has assigned her to your special case. She may be hearing your questions, but she is also listening for further instructions from Him. She is tuned in, both horizontally—establishing a relationship with you, the mentoree—and vertically—awaiting further instructions as to what precious nugget the Lord is placing in her heart for you.

Throughout your life, although you may not recognize them at the time, there will be major and minor mentors who are sent for a season—a Sunday school teacher, a Scout leader, some godly woman in your church or community, an older woman who understands how to begin where you are and is equipped to impart what is needed for *now.* These unknown mentors will spark something in your spirit that will cause you to dig deeper.

As a child camping in the high country of North Carolina, I experienced the thrill of panning for gold in a cold, clear mountain stream. The minute a shaft of light, filtered through a canopy of trees, would strike certain rocks, the glint of gold alerted all my senses and I just knew there was a gold mine under there! I would dig feverishly, hoping to be the one to find the mother lode buried in the earth since the beginning of time.

Mentors ignite your spiritual senses to the possibility of all that God has placed in you. They are sent to help you mine the treasure that has been there all along.

She Offers Gentle Correction

Don't expect your mentor to ignore your faults and emphasize only the positive. As God's appointed ambassador, she has the right to point out any course correction necessary to guide you on the path to righteousness.

No one enjoys being challenged. It is human nature—our old *sin* nature—to resist, even to put up a smokescreen to hide behind. If you are unable to receive correction, your mentor cannot work with you. You will prevent the message from getting through even as it is being delivered.

At such times, it may help to remember that Jesus said, "As many as I *love,* I rebuke and chasten" (Rev. 3:19 NKJV). If you are in a season of "chastening"—the Hebrew word carries the idea of discipline and instruction that seek to lead one away from *eternal* chastisement—this simply proves that you are the beloved of the Lord.[2]

Mentors who offer warnings and admonitions understand this and are being obedient to God's Word:

> God's people must not be quarrelsome; they must be gentle, patient teachers of those who are wrong. Be humble when you are trying to teach those who are mixed up concerning the truth. For if you talk meekly and courteously to them they are more likely, with God's help, to turn away from their wrong ideas and believe what is true.
>
> Then they will come to their senses and escape from Satan's trap of slavery to sin....
>
> 2 Timothy 2:24-26

Remember, God's Word is the plumb line, the scale by which all truth is measured. Why remain in the clutches of the enemy when you can "come to [your] senses...and escape"?

She Will Not Try To Control You

While your mentor will be extremely interested in your progress toward godliness, she will not try to manipulate or micromanage you. She is not a schoolteacher waiting to pop your knuckles when you give the wrong answers. She offers critique, not criticism: "I can see that you are growing in this area." "This is what it will take to move to the next level in your walk with the Lord." "How can I help?"

Since she herself is accountable to the Lord, she will help to keep you accountable as well—with grace and without judgment. She knows you so well—through God's anointing—yet still does not judge you. You can trust her. You believe that she would never betray you nor repeat the confidences you share. Like a tightly wrapped bud relaxing into full blossom, you are free to open up and bloom.

There is freedom in the relationship between a mentor and mentoree. The freedom comes from the mutual understanding that God has placed you in each other's lives *for a very important purpose.* Whether or not you are aware of all that this implies in the beginning, you will be able to sense the special bond between you—unlike even your relationship with your mother, daughter, sister, social acquaintance, or casual friend.

Because your mentor does not force her opinions, you are eager to hear more. She drops little pearls of wisdom at just the right time, like tiny seeds scattered upon the soil of your soul. Further counsel produces gentle showers that water her words and enable them to take root. Her wisdom is bestowed as softly as a whisper, which you can hear perfectly. It is a gentle nudge in the right direction. *You know her words are God's voice speaking truth, freeing you to be all He intended you to be.*

God's words of truth through her will make you free. Free to discover who you are in Him. Free to embrace yourself with your flaws and faults. Free to forgive yourself without self-condemnation or guilt. Free to revel in this new perception of yourself—God's view of you as seen through the eyes of your mentor. Free to move on. Free to change. Free to grow.

She Is Able To Discern Your Potential

The English gatekeeper held all the keys to the places we most wanted to explore on our visit, but he withheld entry on that occasion—for a very good reason. He knew something we didn't know.

Your mentor knows something about you that you don't know about yourself. Don't panic! She may be able to see you with objectivity; but she will see you in your highest light, beyond your present state to the finished product—who you are going to become.

That kind of "knowing" takes discernment and revelation knowledge. Only God can reveal what lies ahead, and He has many creative methods of sharing that revelation with you.

My eighth-grade English teacher was also my Girl Scout leader. In helping us achieve our citizenship merit badges, she was attempting to instill the qualities of good leadership in her sixteen troop members. "I'm going to describe a person who exemplifies an ideal citizen," she said, "and when I get through, I want you to write down who you think it might be."

We picked up our pencils. Already, thinking big, I suspected she might describe some prominent person from our nation's history—or maybe even God or Jesus Himself. After deity, my hierarchy included the founding fathers and all the presidents of the United States. I couldn't wait to guess!

"This person is honest," she began, "never fails to be kind, encourages others, always shares, and is involved in church and community activities."

Well, it *could* be President Washington or President Lincoln. They were both extremely honest. George Washington told the truth about chopping down the cherry tree, and President Lincoln once walked several miles to return a penny. But it was too early to be sure of the answer. I needed more clues.

"I've never known this person to be selfish, always waiting her turn, not pushing to the front of the line. She is a team player...."

Well, it certainly wasn't one of the founding *fathers!* This person was a *"she"!* My teacher had said so.

"She is always willing to help others earn their badges. In fact, she is sitting right here in this room."

Oh, so it was one of *us*. Wide-eyed, we glanced around, wondering which of us was the model citizen our leader had just profiled. Thinking long and hard, we made our choices, wrote down the names, and handed our papers to the teacher.

After she had tallied the votes, she stood there for a moment with a knowing smile, eyes dancing. "You will be pleased to learn that, with only two exceptions, every vote was for Ann Williams."

My mouth dropped open. I sat stunned, too surprised to breathe. I hadn't a clue it would be *me!*

I share this story only because that day was a major revelation to me, a turning point. It would take twenty years—when I had passed through some deep waters, had reached a certain level of spiritual maturity, and was in business for myself—before I would understand the total significance of that moment. The strong message my teacher sent was that I possessed, even then, some leadership traits and a quality of life that would open doors of opportunity to me and that I needed to guard them and use them wisely. She was mining gold that day—and the buried treasure lay within my own spirit.

What words have been spoken over your life? *Through God's grace and mercy, the negative messages can be erased. Consider the positive.* What truth resounded clearly in your heart? In looking back, can you find past mentors who went undiscovered until you were mature enough to recognize them for the part they would play in your future?

Each mentor is sent for a season. During the mentorship she is especially accessible and influential, but she may ultimately be a presence throughout your entire life. Look for her. The bond you form today will never be broken.

CHAPTER 3

Accessing the Path of Righteousness

Heaven can be entered only through the narrow gate! The highway to hell is broad, and its gate is wide enough for all the multitudes who choose its easy way. But the Gateway to Life is small, and the road is narrow, and only a few ever find it.

MATTHEW 7:13,14

It was a setup by the enemy of my soul. We met at a college fraternity party. He was the best dancer, the cutest and most popular boy there by far. Newly released from my father's house with its comforts and securities, my life was one big ball, spinning faster and faster out of control.

Compared to the confinement of home and church with all those traditions and restrictions, this was pure heaven. I had put the Lord out of my life and was doing my own thing. Young and vulnerable, sheltered and inexperienced, I was enticed by the trappings of glamour and freedom, pirouetted past the turn in the road, and danced all the way to Egypt! I married the handsome prince, but there was no happy-ever-after ending to our love story.

Swept Away

The enemy's camp is beautifully decorated. Music is playing so you can't hear the sounds of silent screams. The lights are dimmed, hiding tragic faces behind the masks. All lines are blurred, indistinct, surreal. It's no wonder the young, in particular, often are swept away by the way things appear to be and find themselves captives in a foreign land.

So how do we find the path to what's real and lasting—and why do we miss it so often? I believe God's Word is a map that clearly points out the road to righteousness.

Broadway: The Highway to Hell

In Matthew's version of the Good News of Jesus Christ, we find two choices, a kind of crossroads—a broad road and a narrow one. It's the intersection at Broadway and Narrowgate. (Matt. 7:13,14.) In my designer's eye, my imagination runs wild when I read this passage.

Broadway is big. I can envision a wide entryway, beckoning the passerby to step inside. The spacious surroundings will easily accommodate a large crowd, baggage and all. This is the politically correct road and the one the "in" crowd is traveling. You'll find pride and arrogance, unbelief, gluttony, lust, and disobedience to God on this road.

Broadway is bright. The lighting over this gate is artfully designed to call attention to the entry point. Consequently, no one can miss it! Satan "can change himself into an angel of light" (2 Cor. 11:14), and that light is an illusion.

Broadway is beautiful. This thoroughfare is quite appealing to the eye and individually styled for a variety of tastes. Does your ego need stroking? Broadway will boost your self-esteem to rock-star proportions—at least temporarily. Are you looking for love? The wide place with its seductive attractions offers a smorgasbord of choices that stimulate without satisfying. Do you crave approval, applause, celebrity, possessions? It's all here for the asking.

Jesus, too, was tempted by the superficial: "Satan took him to the peak of a very high mountain and showed him the nations of the world and all their glory. 'I'll give it all to you,' Satan said, 'if you will only kneel and worship me'" (Matt. 4:8,9).

Jesus didn't fall for that old line, as I did in my first marriage. Jesus was too plugged in to the Word of God. He *was* the Word of God! "'Get out of here, Satan,' Jesus told him. 'The Scriptures say, "Worship only the Lord God. Obey him"'" (v. 10).

The antidote to temptation—the way to snuff out the fiery darts of the enemy—is the Word. Know it and use it to parry those offensive blows. If I had only known the Author of the Book more intimately, I would have been able to find my way to Him sooner. Instead, I found myself in a hellish far country—in bondage to my own wrong choices. Fear set in. It was a place of blackness and bleakness, a destination of destruction. I didn't plan to stay there—not for another minute!

Narrowgate: The Highway to Holiness

The narrow gate leading to heaven is not easy to find. The gate is rusty from disuse, and only a few die-hards will make the effort to look for it. Before you can enter, you must leave all baggage behind. And once inside, the path leads uphill through rocky terrain. It doesn't sound very inviting, yet it is essential that we learn how to access this area. It is as important as life and death.

When I married my college sweetheart—for all the wrong reasons—I enjoyed the pleasures of sin for a season (Heb. 11:25); but the day of reckoning came, and I found myself abandoned with two small daughters and no job. It was during that time of awakening that I began to look for the narrow gate again.

It wasn't that I had lost my salvation. As a child I was saved during a Billy Graham crusade, was brought up in a mainstream denominational church, and knew the Lord—at least I knew *about* Him. I could quote Scripture, discuss doctrine with some degree of intelligence, and was at church every time the doors were open; but I was as empty as a crystal vase waiting to be filled with a lovely bouquet of flowers.

Simply stated, I had veered off course and strayed into the world, where I found no mercy, no grace. I wanted to find the path that leads straight to the throne of God, back to my Father's house, but first there were a few hard lessons in store.

Narrowgate is a place of discipline. I've never really cared for the word *discipline.* It sounds like detention, time out, or raps on the knuckles with a rod of correction. It seems ominous and dreary. The truth of the matter is that *discipline* is from the root word *disciple* or *learner.*[1] To be disciplined is to receive instruction.[2]

Having married before completing college, I was qualified for no work. The two little girls and I moved to Atlanta right after the divorce so that I could attend the art institute there. Armed with a degree, I would surely land a good job and be able to provide for my family. Either that, or I would have to admit defeat and go home to Daddy.

Actually, returning to South Carolina was never really an option. I needed to prove—if only to myself—that I was perfectly capable of standing on my own two feet. Ill prepared as I was for adulthood, I would not depend on my parents, nor would I marry for financial security. There would be no shortcuts. I had made my bed. Now I would lie in it until I found a way out.

While looking at some newly decorated model condominiums one day, I happened to meet the real estate agent on site: a gentleman with snow-white hair and the affable manner of a grandfather. He commented more on the girls' decorum than on their matching outfits and perky ponytails. I, of course, was pleased that he had noticed.

Suddenly, out of the blue, he asked me to critique the models we were visiting. Why would a real estate agent care about the opinion of someone barely out of design school? "Well," I began, somewhat hesitantly, "if you asked ten designers, you'd get ten different opinions. The creative process is not an exact science. I believe I'd suggest two conversation groups instead of one in this room, and I'd dim the lights for a warmer ambiance."

When he asked for my card, I told him I was not in business, tore out a check deposit slip, handed it to him, and promptly forgot all about it.

Three days later the telephone rang. "I so enjoyed meeting you," came the masculine voice on the other end of the line. "You're one of the most charming people I've met in a long time." Thinking this was possibly an obscene telephone call, I was about to slam down the receiver when he chuckled. "Oh, I *am* sorry. I should have introduced myself. I met you at some model townhouses and loved your ideas. I've taken the liberty of setting up a meeting with our financial backers. They need someone with your keen eye and astute business sense for a new project."

Oh, so this was not just *any* real estate agent. I learned that the charming man had recommended my design services to his investors.

Suddenly a Scripture verse I had hidden away years before burst into remembrance—the one about entertaining angels unaware. (Heb. 13:2.)

I also learned that *sometimes God sends mentors for a moment*. He used this man in a huge way to set me back on course and establish me in a business that I could operate out of my home. And in the next few years, in the classroom of the Spirit, I would learn more about interior design—both in the physical world and in the spiritual realm—than any university, art institute, or Bible course might have taught me. But the lessons would not come easily.

Narrowgate is a place of persecution. In the Greek language, the word for narrow is *thlipsis,* which means "tribulation."[3] I can identify! I'll bet you can too. Yet my early sufferings came about because of a decision of my own foolish heart and stubborn will. The kind of tribulation Jesus was teaching on in His eloquent sermon is the result of a conscious surrender to the will of God.

It's this kind of encouragement that James offers: "Is your life full of difficulties and temptations? Then be happy, for when the way is rough, your patience has a chance to grow. So let it grow, and don't try to squirm out of your problems. For when your patience is finally in full bloom, then you will be ready for anything, strong in character, full and complete" (James 1:2-4).

By the time I as a single mother had chased two active girls, made it through design school, and launched my business, I felt more like a wilted petunia than a woman in full bloom! I suppose I did develop character and patience as well as a readiness for anything.

As the only divorced person in my church in the early '70s, I was an embarrassment. They didn't know what to do with me. The poor lady who was trying to help me get situated hemmed and hawed, feverishly casting about for some way to explain the predicament, yet was very sensitive to the fact that I needed a place. I didn't fit with the singles because I had been married. I didn't fit in with the married couples because I was no longer a married woman. So I was allowed to choose where I would be most comfortable. I chose to teach fifth graders in Sunday school.

Little did I know that I was walking into the purposeful plan of my heavenly Father, designed to equip me for the next stage of my life. Neither did I know that the means of correction and shaping would come in the form of a gentle persecutor, a little girl who diligently challenged my theology each Sunday. "Doesn't that verse mean...?" she would begin.

When she spoke, her voice was almost prophetic. I recognized the ring of truth when I heard it. Spurred on by my small mentor, I poured over the Scriptures each Saturday evening, determined not to be outdone. Not even Grandmother Williams had so motivated me! This authoritative little person became a revealer, and I began to receive spiritual guidance. Now I know that mentors come in all sizes, shapes, colors—and ages.

Narrowgate is a place of limitations and boundaries. Who would have thought that entrance to the narrow way would be so difficult? Once you have finally found it and are determined to follow through, it shouldn't be such a tight spot. Right? Wrong. The narrow gate opens to an ongoing upward struggle—with infinite rewards both now and for all eternity.

For one thing, the restrictive nature of Narrowgate is a kind of protection. You dare not wander far from the path for fear of falling off into some deep ravine. No, best to stay very near your Guide, the only One who knows the area completely because He created it. The upward journey builds spiritual muscle, and soon you are able to accomplish more than you ever thought possible.

The Holy Spirit is just waiting to be tapped to enable, equip, and encourage. It is He who leads you into all truth. (John 16:13.) I was more and more eager to be led.

Enter Eliza

It was a father of our country, Abraham Lincoln, who quoted the old proverb, "When the student is ready, the teacher will come."

It is our Father in heaven who sends companions along the way to inspire and to encourage, to mentor and to meddle! One profoundly wise woman was to be the next member of that faculty. I met her after landing my first design job: a country club.

"Is this the talented Ann Cloer who transformed the club?" The voice on the other end of the line was cultured and refined, spoken in a soft southern drawl. "My husband and I have just combined two homes and are in need of some design help."

Even before our appointment, scheduled for later in the week, I sensed that I was about to embark on a journey from which there would be no return. The confirmation came when we met in person and exchanged greetings. From her piercing, steel-blue eyes to her elegant attire and gracious manner, I knew that I was in the presence of someone very special. The next words from her lips stunned me: "Are you a Christian?"

When I assured her that I was, she insisted on hearing all about it. As I looked into her wise eyes and told my story, I knew that something was connecting at a very deep level. I felt immediately at home with her, as if I'd known her all my life. She seemed to have the ability to hear my heart. This was far more than a business engagement or a social outing. Our meeting was a divine appointment.

When God sends a mentor, all circuits will be operational. Emanating from this gracious woman was godly love, encouragement, genuine interest, a desire to impart knowledge and wisdom. As we continued to chat—more about spiritual things than her need of my professional services—she said something that I shall never forget. It was a word straight from God that would change my life from that moment on. She said, "God has so much more for you than you've ever imagined. He has a powerful plan for your life."

The prophetic seed she planted that day pierced my heart. She was breathing life into dead dreams, nurturing a small shoot of hope that had been languishing in some dark corner of my spirit. Although I didn't fully understand all that was taking place, I knew I needed to pay attention to everything this woman said. God must have heard my desperate pleas and sent this deep well from which I could draw life-giving water. I could not know that day just how deep I was being prepared to go.

Something More

With Eliza's dramatic entry into my life, I knew this was a huge second chance for me—not only professionally but spiritually. Hungry for more, I began attending a Bible study that she and her husband held each Wednesday evening in their home. With the same passion I have for my work, I devoured every crumb of knowledge they imparted; but it was Eliza to whom my heart was tuned.

Each shopping expedition for fabric swatches or furnishings for their new home was an occasion to learn more about the Lord whom I had spurned earlier in my life. Viewed through Eliza's penetrating eyes, He became visible to me, not as One who takes away our good times, but as the only One who fully satisfies and brings us more joy than our cups can contain. "I have come that [you] may have life, and that you may have it more abundantly" (John 10:10 NKJV). Daily I was falling more and more in love with Jesus!

There was even more. At the time my bond with Eliza was fully cemented in place, she issued an invitation to attend a spiritual retreat in a wonderful old hotel south of Atlanta. The place oozed with southern charm: framed magnolia prints on the walls, fine dining, yet no television or outside interference.

Mother, ever the "adventuress," was there with me, and we would be rooming with two other women assigned by our hostess. We quickly unpacked and strolled the grounds, taking in the beauty and peace of our surroundings.

The first session that evening began with singing and worship. Although I had been a church member most of my life, I had never experienced anything quite like this. Everyone's eyes were closed and many lifted their hands—except for Mother and me. I don't know what Mother must have been thinking, but I began to observe that these people were communing with God. It all seemed very personal and real.

As they sang, we attempted to follow along, though the words were unfamiliar. Still, something was stirring in my soul. Intrigued by all that Eliza had taught me, for weeks my daily prayer had been, "Lord, reveal Yourself. Guide my life. I can't do it anymore without You."

After the brief message, delivered by a young evangelist, there was an altar call. In his twinkling eyes was the same look I had seen in Eliza's. "Have you prayed to receive salvation?" he asked us. Well, I didn't need that. He certainly wasn't speaking to me. I knew all about salvation and had accepted Jesus into my heart at an early age.

Are you sure you have everything you need from Me, Ann? I heard an unmistakably still, small voice whispering across my spirit. *If My children love Me, they will obey me.*

I squirmed a little, feeling too warm even though I was wearing a sundress on this summer evening. "Are you ready to receive all that the Lord has for you?" the evangelist was asking.

When Eliza gently put her hands on my shoulders and gave me a motherly push, I found myself at the front of the room, hands lifted! With his hand on my head, the man leaned forward, praying with great conviction, "Lord, You hear Your child. Fill her with Your Holy Spirit and every gifting You have for her."

At that moment I felt a warm, thick substance—like oil or heavy perfume—pouring over my head. *Surely he wouldn't do something like that!* I thought. My eyes were closed, but the substance—whatever it was—continued to run down my face and onto my shoulders. I peeked, crossing my eyes to look at my nose. Glancing down at my shoulder, I could see no visible sign of anything. Yet the warm flow persisted until it covered my entire body. What could this possibly be?

"Now open your eyes and say whatever word comes to mind, no matter how ridiculous it may sound." All of a sudden a strange, non-sensical word came to mind and, wanting to be obedient, I spoke it aloud. When I finally returned to my seat, Mother commented under her breath, "Some of these people are speaking Japanese. I recognize it from my travels there. I believe everyone in this room is speaking a different language. Why, I do believe they're speaking in tongues!"

Whatever they called it, I knew it was real. It had happened to me! Later my roommate explained the phenomenon I had experienced. "You went through deliverance. God has filled you with the oil of joy (Isa. 61:3) and brought you into a new place." I could barely

sleep all night, still enjoying the afterglow of that encounter with the Lord. I knew very little about the Spirit life I had entered, but I did know He was alive in me.

I went off like a rocket! Like Peter, and fueled by Eliza's mentoring role in my life, I stepped out of my safe little denominational boat and took a step toward my destiny.

CHAPTER 4

Beware: Wolves in "Cheap" Clothing

*Beware of false teachers who come disguised as
harmless sheep, but are wolves and will tear you apart.
You can detect them by the way they act, just as you
can identify a tree by its fruit.... The way to identify
a tree or a person is by the kind of fruit produced.*

MATTHEW 7,15,16,20

As an experienced interior designer for over twenty-seven years,
my eyes have been trained to recognize the real. Put me in a room
filled with priceless antiques and reproductions, and I can spot the
difference between the authentic period piece and the carefully
crafted copy every time.

This ability did not come naturally or quickly. In design school, I
pored over volumes on the history of furniture. More importantly, I
am part of an industry where daily I am exposed to the finest in furnishings, antique rugs, art, and accessories. Every sense is trained to
select the best for my clients. To run my hand over an exquisite eigh-
teenth century desk gleaming with the patina of time and care is to
experience its provenance. Such pieces bring substance and credibility to the home in which they are placed, and their value only

increases with the years. Therefore, it is easy to see why I am not deceived by an imitation: I know the real thing!

Unfortunately, what is true of the material world is also true in the spiritual realm. Occasionally impostors, strategically placed to deceive and mislead, masquerade as mentors, teachers, and prophets. Beneath the veneer of religiosity, they mimic the truth. Deception is not always easy to detect. False mentors may look good and sound good. But there is one sure way to distinguish them from true mentors: *Avoid anyone who does not acknowledge Jesus Christ as Lord or direct you to the Word of God for confirmation of her instruction.*

Dearly loved friends, don't always believe everything you hear just because someone says it is a message from God: test it first to see if it really is. For there are many false teachers around, and the way to find out if their message is from the Holy Spirit is to ask: Does it really agree that Jesus Christ, God's Son, actually became man with a human body? If so, then the message is from God. If not, the message is not from God....

1 John 4:1-3

If you are seeking someone to encourage you, to reveal truth to you, and to nurture you, beware of these wolves in "cheap" clothing. Look at the fruit of their lives. Do they mirror Jesus Christ?

The Green-Eyed "Monstress"

Some women will never be qualified to mentor because of a jealous, unhealed spirit. For them, it would be difficult to see someone else do well, to be transformed and used by God. A successful mentoree could actually become a threat to this would-be mentor!

A true mentor, on the other hand, is willing to impart rich treasures of wisdom and knowledge without a thought of the return on the investment. She desires to bring out the best in others and is the first to applaud any spiritual achievement.

Part of the reason for God's favor on my business is the fact that I am a team player. In my profession, I have come to recognize my gifts and to enjoy the benefits of the strengths others bring to a decorating project. I don't attempt to assume the role of the architect, but stick to my own area of expertise. When everyone does his or her job well, the result is a lovely home that brings joy to those who dwell there. It is even more fulfilling when I can encourage younger designers in my field and see them excel.

The most effective spiritual mentors will also train their mentorees to go beyond their own ministry. Elisha received a "double portion" of Elijah's anointing. (2 Kings 2:9 KJV.) Esther was crowned queen while her Uncle Mordecai coached her from the shadows. (See the book of Esther.) The apostle John made way for Jesus when he said, "Someone is coming who is greater by far than I am—for he existed long before I did!" (John 1:15).

The jealous spirit demands preferential treatment. I tell my friends that if they ever see *me* acting like that, they have permission to jerk me upside down! If that's *your* problem, get pastoral counseling, and pray for deliverance: "Create in me a new, clean heart, O God, filled with clean thoughts and right desires" (Ps. 51:10).

Mentors must stay under correction at all times. Daily tests will reveal areas of weakness and vulnerability that must be confessed, but the green-eyed "monstress" will not be quick to change.

The Ear-Tickler

This woman will tell you what you want to hear. She is the gusher, extravagant praiser, and flatterer. Basically self-seeking and spoiled, she is a people-pleaser, out for personal gain.

The ear-tickler is after something you *have* or something you *are.* She is not interested in discovering *your* gifts and promoting God's agenda for kingdom purposes. Her aim is personal fame.

My good friend Martha tells of a woman who was just the opposite of this profile. She writes, "It is so empowering to have someone in your life who is not only a mentor, but also your biggest cheerleader, someone who will listen to an unedited heart, yet not publish it abroad. Bertie gave me courage to step out of the boat, out of my safe place, to go deeper with the Lord. When I go through a time of discouragement, I know if she were still here (Bertie died several years ago), she would be rooting for me, telling me that if I will trust the Lord, He will uphold me and ultimately see me through. I do not believe there was a success in my life that she did not celebrate."

While an ear-tickler will not dare speak the hard word, a true mentor will risk the relationship in order to admonish or correct you gently. The Word is clear on this point:

> Let God train you, for he is doing what any loving father does for his children. Whoever heard of a son [daughter] who was never corrected?
>
> Hebrews 12:7

If you are serious about a deeper walk with the Lord, you will welcome correction and learn from it, as my friend Martha did.

"Miss Devil": The Jezebel Spirit

You've surely met Jezebel. The twenty-first century model may look like a fashion plate with no visible flaws, but she reeks of manipulation and control. She's the type who speaks her mind, insists on having her own way, and often causes dissension in her church, community, and friendships.

The biblical Jezebel was rebellious, godless, and a would-be murderess. (See 1 Kings 16 through 2 Kings 11.) She even tried to kill a prophet! She was the ultimate schemer and conniver.

A truly evil woman, Jezebel corrupted her husband, King Ahaz, in such a way that he influenced the entire nation of Israel to worship Baal, a pagan god. During their reign, many of God's prophets were slaughtered. (1 Kings 18:1-4.) It was the prophet Elijah, that great hero of the faith, whom Jezebel personally set out to exterminate on Mount Carmel. What a contest: 850 prophets of Baal versus one lone advocate of Jehovah—a spectacular display of God's providence!

Miss Devil controls everyone around her. There is no end to this woman's quest for control, power, and money. One modern-day Jezebel once led a prayer group composed of a large number of women. A former beauty queen, she was vain and haughty and dictated the agenda of the prayer times, including the length of prayers! It was all about *her*. She ultimately lost her voice and was no longer able to lead. Through pride and control, she forfeited the original call of God on her life and lost her usefulness in ministry.

The Hair-Cutter

A "Delilah" discovers your weakness and uses it against you. Like the cunning and beautiful spy who enticed the strong man,

Samson, to reveal the secret of his strength (his long hair), she kisses and tells. (Judges 16:4-22.) She may claim to be your friend and may even ask for your help and counsel; yet after she has gained the information or contacts she needs, she will turn on you.

Shortly after I married John, a retired business executive who helped heal my heart after my painful first marriage, he sat me down and gave me his perspective on one of my friends, a woman I had helped personally and professionally. I had given her leads and every benefit of my knowledge and expertise in my field.

I was totally unprepared for John's candid appraisal of my situation. "I feel I need to warn you," he said tentatively. "I know this is a delicate matter, but I believe this relationship is potentially dangerous."

I frowned. *What in the world was he talking about? My history with this woman was long and time-tested*—or so I thought. John's people skills were impeccable, so I was willing to listen.

"You're paying her too much for the amount of business she's bringing in," he went on. "If you put her on commission, you may see another side of her." Reluctantly I agreed. A few weeks later, my husband's prophetic insight proved painfully true. Furious over this change in the status of our working relationship, the woman left and did everything she could to destroy my reputation. Thank the Lord, she didn't ask to cut my hair. She would have snatched me bald!

I was blinded by my immaturity and trust at the time and my willingness to give assistance to anyone in need. She used her charm to get what she wanted, and, like Samson, I fell for it. I accepted my "friend" as I perceived her to be. She was anything *but* a friend. She was a deceiver, not a receiver.

The Religious Spirit

I grew up in a wonderful denomination where the Bible was treasured and taught. I will be forever grateful for my spiritual roots. Yet a time came when I began to think more globally, past denominational boundaries and barriers to the greater kingdom of God. After the baptism of the Holy Spirit, I left the church of my childhood.

Set free, I now felt a hunger and thirst for the things of the Lord. Though I had been a pew-sitter for most of my life, content to be spoon-fed the milk of the Word, I now desired to feast on all the riches He had for me.

The danger in seeking a mentor who is locked into traditionalism is that she may not see the bigger picture of all that God is doing in the world.

At the same time, a critical, judgmental spirit can go both ways. True mentors model the virtues set forth in Galatians 5:22-23: "When the Holy Spirit controls our lives he will produce this kind of fruit in us: love, joy, peace, patience, kindness, goodness, faithfulness, gentleness and self-control."

Apparently when I began my deeper walk with God, I, too, was caught up in the old mindset of manmade rules and restrictions. During a prayer meeting in which several hundred people were participating, the leader—one of my major mentors, Mary Crum—suggested that we turn around and take the hand of someone we did not know. As the Lord led, we were to speak a prophetic word over that person.

When I turned, I was surprised to see a gentleman who looked a lot like Santa Claus—beautiful snow-white, neatly clipped beard and all. His gaze was kind and gentle, but it seemed as if he could see right through me. "You go first," he said.

Still new at this kind of thing, I prayed and spoke the word I believed the Lord was giving me for him. Then it was his turn. Very lightly, but deliberately, he placed his hand on my forehead and began, "In the name of Jesus, I call out that religious spirit."

Stunned by this declaration, my eyes popped open. As he prophesied a sweet word over me, I sensed the presence of the Lord. The man spoke with such calm authority that I was determined to find out who he was and was startled to learn that he was the chief deliverance pastor in Atlanta! God loved me so much that He had sent a special ambassador of His mercy to deliver me from the spirits that would hinder His call on my life.

He will do the same for you. The religious spirit will say, "Do only the things your denomination sanctions." The Lord says, "I have a treasure chest for you. There is so much more. If you will seek Me, I will open the floodgates of heaven and pour you out a blessing so that there is not room enough to receive it!" (Mal. 3:10, author's paraphrase.)

The Devil in Disguise (Witchcraft)

Some of the "current" trends in health and recreation are straight from the pit of hell. For those who are distressed, distraught, and confused about the future, these strategies may seem made to order: Yoga, tarot cards, Ouija boards, fortune-telling, psychic readings, horoscopes, spirit guides, channeling, crystals, and so many others. Sound like fun? Make no mistake about it: These mind games are anything but innocent—they are deadly.

The devil doesn't play games! "Be careful—watch out for attacks from Satan, your great enemy. He prowls around like a hungry, roaring lion, looking for some victim to tear apart" (1 Peter 5:8).

If you question any of these practices, check God's Word for His opinion: "There shall not be found among you anyone who...practices witchcraft, or a soothsayer [fortune-teller],...or one who conjures spells, or a medium, or a spiritualist, or one who calls up the dead. For all who do these things are an abomination to the Lord" (Deut. 18:10-12 NKJV). *Abomination?* Yes. That's just how disgusting these "innocent" pastimes are to the Lord God Almighty.

Proud Babylon, once a great civilization, fell because of this very sin. The Lord said:

> You felt secure in all your wickedness.... Your "wisdom" and "knowledge" have caused you to turn away from me and claim that you yourself are Jehovah.
>
> Call out the demon hordes you've worshiped all these years. Call on them to help you.... You have advisors by the ton—your astrologers and stargazers, who try to tell you what the future holds. But they are as useless as dried grass burning in the fire. They cannot even deliver themselves!
>
> Isaiah 47:10,12-14

Please listen to me. Anything or anyone you look to for direction outside of God's Word is off limits to the believer. That's why it is so important to be grounded in the Word, to study and seek, to pray for wisdom and discernment before making a decision about a mentor or mentoree.

You must learn to be discerning, or the devil will eat your lunch. He will persuade you to be tolerant and politically correct. He will try to nullify your witness until you're lukewarm about everything—and you know what Jesus had to say about lukewarm church members. (Rev. 3:15,16.)

The enemy will even accuse you of being judgmental, when judgment is a huge part of wisdom! It is our business as mentors and mentorees to judge the fruit of the Spirit, the gifts of the Spirit, and the truth as opposed to error or imbalance in the body of Christ.

For example, some people are so afraid of the next move of God that they hinder themselves from moving on. When the spirit of laughter was first manifesting itself, John and I were propped up on pillows in bed, watching a TV evangelist. Behind him, in the choir, a woman started laughing hysterically. The evangelist didn't bat an eye and kept on preaching. I sat up straighter in bed, squinting in disbelief. "Why in the world are they letting that woman do that on national TV?" I asked John.

About that time, a woman in the second row fell over laughing. "They must have devils all over that church!" I said. "How rude and intrusive. I can't believe they're showing this. No way is this God."

I probably could have counted to three before the spirit of laughter hit me like a ton of bricks, and I doubled up, holding my sides. "It's real!" I told John breathlessly. "It's real!" By this time, I could barely speak because I was laughing so hard. "Well, whatever they've got, you've got," he said, laughing with me.

How precious of the Lord to confirm this phenomenon personally. Every time I think I have the formula figured out, God shows me a different twist. What He does for me, He will do for you. Just trust Him.

The Midnight Caller

Some women are so needy that they latch on to the nearest support system and invade boundaries. These time-stealers thoughtlessly disrupt family time, rehash the same old story over and over, disturb your sleep, and otherwise wear down a potential mentor.

That is why it is absolutely essential that prayer precede any new mentoring relationship. Even if confirmation is given that God is truly in the situation, it is a good thing to lay down some basic ground rules for spiritual etiquette:

- The Golden Rule covers most bases: "Do unto others as you would have them do unto you" (Matt. 7:12).

- Suggest a beginning and a cutoff point for prayer and counseling sessions.

- Keep the conversation on track.

- Avoid gossip and other ungodly time-wasters.

- For the mentor: Build in time for rest and personal refreshing with the Lord. Even Jesus, who gave away everything He had to others, sometimes found it necessary to retreat for prayer and solitude. "He went out into the mountains to pray, and prayed all night" (Luke 6:12).

Truth—Or Consequences

We never fully estimate the power of our personal platform. I am just so grateful that during my prodigal years, I did not have great visibility, or I might have seriously hindered the work of the kingdom. In God's divine timing, He brought me fully back to Him and sent me godly mentors before launching me in ministry. He does not send us out unprepared.

I still look to Eliza as a general in God's army. I still pay attention to everything she says. She is so fresh, so non-controlling, so encouraging, so centered on prayer and God's Word. Never in all the twenty-five years I have known her has she said, "Ann, this is what you need to do." Instead, she has said, "I am praying about that for you," or "Ann, you need to pray and ask the Lord to show you." She has not given me the answers; she has pointed me to the Answer.

When you have met the true, the authentic—like Eliza and Mary and others I will introduce to you in this book—it is much less difficult to spot a fake. This is how you can determine the real thing:

- Listen to her words. Do they line up with the Word of God?

- Look at her walk. Is she an example of godly living?

- Is God confirming that this woman has been sent to mentor you for a season?

- Is she committed to prayer?

If the answers to these questions are not an emphatic yes, then turn and run in the opposite direction! Do not submit yourself to someone who has not been sent.

CHAPTER 5

Closing the Gate

To everything there is a season,
a time for every purpose under heaven:
A time to embrace, and a time to refrain from embracing.

ECCLESIASTES 3:1,5 NKJV

Why hasn't she called? What could I possibly have done to offend her?

These and other tormenting questions raced through my head each time I thought of my beloved friend and mentor. For some reason, the one I had relied on to impart wisdom and revelation to me was suddenly and unaccountably absent from my life. I was devastated!

Although I would run into Eliza occasionally and the old affection seemed intact, her behavior was puzzling. My love and need for her were as acute as ever and I missed our former closeness terribly, but something between us had shifted. It didn't make any sense at all. I stayed before the Lord for several years, asking what I had done wrong. If she had died, my grief could not have been more raw.

Many mentors later, the truth finally became obvious to me. It was simply this: A season had ended, and the Lord was bringing me to another level, a greater vision than I could have dreamed or imagined. While Eliza's ministry was foundational to my faith and I thrived on the spiritual support she offered, I did not know how to say goodbye when the mentoring season had ended. Eliza, on the other hand, was like the mother bird who pushes her baby out of the nest. She wanted me to try my wings—and fly!

A Time To Let Go

It is human nature to want to keep our friendships and relationships at white-hot intensity. Maybe we'd love for marriage to be a perpetual first-love feeling, or perhaps each of us would like to be the only one to whom a friend tells her deepest secrets. But life has its hills and valleys, its peaks and pits and seasons.

The mentoring relationship is no different. The experience of receiving truth from a trusted mentor is intense while it is occurring. The discoveries of your spiritual gifts, new revelation about God—all this is heady stuff. You don't want to lose that sense of heightened awareness, the thrill of exploring new territory. It is as precious as gold.

God never intended for any person—mentor, mate, or friend—to be the revealer of all truth. That's the job description of the Holy Spirit. By divine design, we are limited in our ability to nurture each other. If it were possible for us to reveal all truth, we would not need *Him!*

"Beware lest you break the contract the Lord your God has made with you!... He is a devouring fire, a jealous God" (Deut. 4:23,24). "I am Jehovah your God.... You may worship no other god than me...for I, the Lord your God, am very possessive. I will not share your affection with any other god!" (Ex. 20:2,3,5). He loves you so much that He jealously guards your special relationship with Him—even when that relationship is one He has designed, such as marriage or mentoring!

When the mentoring season ends, the purpose has been completed and the anointing lifts for that relationship. In retrospect, that is exactly what was happening with Eliza and me. My problem was rejection. Having suffered the abandonment of a husband, this felt very much like the same thing—losing someone precious to my heart.

Yet as I matured, I would learn to view each mentor who comes and goes as the blessing she is and not hold on too tightly or too long. This precious woman of God taught me the power of prayer and the importance of searching God's Word for truth. I learned so much from her, but His plan for me was greater than any single person.

After that fallow season when all communication stopped, the level of our relationship changed. Despite our age difference, we became more like peers, giving and receiving equally. Fifteen minutes with Eliza can carry me for a year.

I now know, all these years later, that the time had come for Eliza to move on to her next protégé; I, to my next mentor.

Saints With a Specialty

Each mentor comes with her own spiritual specialty. Her contribution to your life will be as unique as fingerprints or snowflakes or sands on the seashore, for your destiny is yours alone, ordained before the foundations of the world.

Your next mentor will:

- Deliver an impartation. This impartation will be God's message for the moment, hand-delivered to you by His chosen vessel.

- Point out the significance of your spiritual gifts and how they fit in with what God is doing in the body of Christ.

- Prepare you to be expanded and stretched for all that He has dreamed for you.

- Escort you to the next level, where you will be ready to receive fresh revelation.

As each woman is brought into your life, you will learn to recognize God's purpose for that relationship. Like a divine recipe for your very personal destiny, you will receive each ingredient just when you need it. One woman may open the gate to understanding forgiveness. Another will model for you the gift of encouragement. Still another may usher you into the realm of the prophetic.

However, if God designed you to be a chocolate cake, He won't send you the ingredients for a coconut pie! Each person is uniquely equipped and qualified to fulfill the purpose for which she was born.

> Some of us have been given the special ability as apostles; to others he has given the gift of being able to preach well; some have special ability in winning people to Christ, helping them to trust him as their Savior' still others have a gift for caring for God's people as a shepherd does his sheep, leading and teaching them in the ways of God.
>
> Why is it that he gives us these special abilities to do certain things best? It is that God's people will be equipped to do better work for him, building up the church, the body of Christ, to a position of strength and maturity.
>
> Ephesians 4:11,12

Mentors help to stir up those abilities—the ingredients—to produce the perfect work that God created you to be.

You will remain with each mentor for a season—whether a moment or a lifetime. Then, after receiving the impartation God has for you through her, you will be ready to move on to the next exciting phase of the journey.

Accepting God's Timing

As Clara liked to say, "God is in no hurry. He owns all the time there is." He may show you something through your mentor that will not be immediately evident to you. Just as a seed shows no signs of life until it germinates, so God's revelation takes time before it is fulfilled. The hurry-up spirit is not the Holy Spirit!

A beautiful flower is first an ugly brown seed, then a bud, then a fully mature bloom. As God's Spirit begins to bud in us and we glimpse His glory, we will become more and more willing to wait. Mother was late with one of her four pregnancies when she asked the doctor, "Has anyone in the history of the world just never delivered the baby?" "No, Miss Margaret," he replied with a twinkle in his eye. "Everyone eventually delivers." It may seem that the waiting will never be over, but God keeps His promises, and the time will come for fulfillment.

Wise mentors know something about timing. They will point out that *if you don't wait, you may miss the very thing the Lord is trying to teach you.* Each moment of your life is full of purpose. There are no vacations with God, no down times. Even weeks of recovery from illness can be used to listen for his still, small voice.

Catherine Marshall, a well-known Christian writer and lecturer, once spent a year in bed, recovering from tuberculosis. While she was flat on her back, she communed with God and experienced His presence in a supernatural moment of revelation. It was the beginning of her healing—a total release from disease that took place as she came to know him more fully in sickness than in health and hectic activity.[1]

We can't go to the deep place in the midst of hustle and bustle. When you surrender your time to the Lord, you are giving Him the essence of who you are. As one of four children, I loved to crawl up in my father's lap and nestle. Daddy always sat in a favorite wingback chair at home, his unlit trademark cigar dangling from his lips and his reading glasses perched over his nose. I loved nothing more than to simply be in his arms, a lap baby. It was a chosen place, a place of privilege. I was his child, his beloved.

In my father's arms, I learned how to be still.

The same is true with our heavenly Father. You are a daughter of the King, a chosen handmaiden. When you come away with Him to the quiet place, He will whisper His secrets to you. He will multiply your time, invigorate you, and take you to places you never dreamed of going. "They that wait upon the Lord shall renew their strength. They shall mount up with wings like eagles; they shall run and not be weary; they shall walk and not faint" (Isa. 40:31).

To mentors, Eliza, the seasoned veteran, says, "Don't be quick to speak for the Lord. Wait on God's intelligence. If He doesn't appoint you, don't do it. If He doesn't send you, don't go. You'll be out there by yourself—and that's a frightening place to be!"

More To Come

It was Eliza, too, who was God's matchmaker. Indirectly, she introduced me to my husband, John Platz, the best gift God ever gave me! She handed me a brochure one night at prayer group and said, "You really ought to take this trip." Intrigued, I glanced down and was surprised to see that it was a promotional piece for a tour of the Holy Land.

On that trip, twenty-two years ago, John and I met and fell in love. Our marriage ever since has been the proverbial "match made in heaven." John was another mentor sent by God. He nourished the tender shoots that sprouted from my earliest mentors and ushered me part of the way into the next stage of spiritual growth.

After we married, and still eager for more of the Lord, I asked Him to reveal His fullness. I had a dream one night, and in this dream, I was slain in the Spirit. Now, not having experienced anything like this in the denomination in which I grew up, this was totally unexpected. The next morning I told John about my dream.

"Oh, you didn't dream it," he informed me matter-of-factly. "It really happened. You woke up yelling. When I put my hand on your forehead, you fell back into the pillows."

This was only one of many other such experiences to follow. Once a powerfully anointed pastor from Africa was speaking to a group of his supporters. I was honored to be among the twelve people to meet with him. He spoke of resurrections in the Third World, of dramatic miracles taking place, of people being healed and raised from the dead. I loved watching him. He was a stunning man with dark, deeply animated features.

Suddenly he stopped and looked at me. "God wants me to minister to you," he said to my immense surprise. As he prayed, binding and commanding spirits to leave me, I sensed an emotional healing. With his hand on my head, I felt as weightless as an astronaut. God met me on the concrete floor, cushioned as if with angels' wings!

If the Lord had spoken aloud, He would have been saying, "Enter into My rest," because I could literally feel the tension draining out of my body, my muscles relaxing. It was the sense of being in my father's lap at Willbrook, his arms around me, comforted and content.

I didn't jump up but allowed the Lord to complete what He had begun. It was a time of taking away the old and filling with new things, an empowering for the future.

The more you relinquish your will, the more the Spirit will reveal Himself to you. Trust Him to bring you the experiences and the people you need. He has promised: "I will send another Comforter to teach you all things and bring much to your remembrance." (John 14:26.)

Short Season

It is possible to mentor a person in nanoseconds. When God sets up the encounter, it doesn't have to take long to accomplish His purpose.

Eliza tells the story of a situation in which she was asked to mentor a woman going through a horrible divorce. Feeling overwhelmed by an already crowded schedule, Eliza resisted the challenge for about three weeks.

On the way home from the grocery store one day, however, she heard the Lord's instruction: *Go by [this woman's] house.* Having lived a life of prayer, she recognized His voice. She tried to argue with Him, reminding Him of her grocery sacks laden with frozen food, but the voice persisted. She obeyed reluctantly.

At the woman's house, Eliza spotted a car in the drive and pulled in behind it; but when she got to the door and knocked, there was no answer. She knocked again. This time the door opened slowly to reveal a disheveled woman, eyes red-rimmed, cheeks blotchy with tears.

"You're here," she said with a sigh. "Come on in."

The woman shuffled to the sofa and sank into the plump cushions. Eliza sat beside her, prayed briefly, and left.

Two days later, the friend who had originally suggested the contact called Eliza. "Would you like to know what you stumbled into at my friend's house the other day?"

"Yes, I would."

"She was sitting on the sofa with a loaded gun to her head when you knocked."

Eliza gasped, too stunned to speak.

"What you also didn't know was that she had hidden the gun under the cushion...*where you were sitting while you prayed!*"

Sometimes mentors are lifesavers whose season begins and ends in a single day!

Between the Not Yet's and the Almost There's

It seems that much of my life as a young woman was lived between the not yet's and the almost there's. I was always waiting for something or someone to fill my thoughts and my time. Restless, charged with energy, and caught up in the whirl of youthful activity, my poor choices led to marriage and motherhood before I really knew what I was doing or who I was. It was only when my two girls and I were abandoned a few years later that I slowed down enough to listen to the Lord. A few years later He led me to Eliza.

She was teaching a Bible study in the home of a friend in a nearby town. I recall vividly how she looked—piercing steel-blue eyes, regal posture, elegant, refined, the epitome of a lovely southern lady. At first glance, I liked everything about her. But there was more, much more—a depth of wisdom that was intriguing to me.

When she spoke, her words were like lightning strikes in my spirit. I knew that she knew. The anointing was so strong and special, the words so right and true. The room was crowded, and I was literally sitting at her feet on the floor, gazing up at this woman who was to impact my life more than any other would. Everything she said was so profound, so connected. I knew that I was hearing a powerful message from God.

In that very moment came a still, small voice: *Enjoy her. You're not always going to have her.* Startled, I jumped. Where had *that* come from? Was something terrible going to happen to Eliza?

For His own reasons, which I may never know until we are reunited in heaven, God gave me fair warning of the end of that mentoring season in that very room—but not before I had been nurtured for several more years. And how I loved being nurtured by the best! Eliza made rich deposits in my life. She helped call out my gifts. She challenged me to read the Scriptures for myself, to pray about everything, and to tell others about Jesus. Then, after she had equipped me, she gently pushed me out of the nest.

When she describes that experience today, I can see that it was as painful for her as it was for me. As she speaks, she demonstrates, extending both graceful, manicured hands and giving a little shove. As she does so, she turns her head and closes her eyes, as if unable to bear seeing her fledgling leave. It is enough to ease a long-time hurt.

But I have learned one more lesson from Eliza. When the season is drawing to a close, it would be less painful for a mentor to release a mentoree with a benediction. I say to my mentorees: "Congratulations, darling, you have graduated! Now go with God wherever He leads you. Keep your spiritual eyes open. Your next mentor is on the way!"

Part 2

THE GARDEN GATE: CULTIVATING YOUR GIFTS

There are diversities of gifts, but the same Spirit....
To one is given the word of wisdom through the Spirit,
to another the word of knowledge through the same
Spirit, to another faith by the same Spirit, to another
gifts of healings by the same Spirit, to another the
workings of miracles, to another prophecy, to another
discerning of spirits, to another different kinds of
tongues, to another the interpretation of tongues.
But one and the same Spirit works all these things,
distributing to each one individually as He wills.

1 CORINTHIANS 12:4,8-11

Helen Keller

I never met Helen Keller, the renowned blind and deaf woman who conquered her silent, dark world with the help of her companion and mentor, Anne Sullivan, but I know of someone who did.

When Miss Keller appeared before the Mississippi State Legislature to champion a bill for the handicapped, Dorothy, a sixth grader at the time, was present with her class. Afterward, her father, who managed the hotel where the great lady was staying, arranged a private interview, where Dorothy added Helen Keller's name— painstakingly hand-written—to her autograph book.

The next day, a newspaper article added to Dorothy's impressions. In that article Miss Keller told of her perception of color: "I interpret color as mental pictures. Pink is like something soft and lovely—a baby's cheek or a rosebud. The color of green is like the overflowing joy of spring. Red means warmth and courage."[1]

An avid reader, Miss Keller said, "The book I read most often and love the most is the Bible. It inspires me for conquest over limitations. It has flowed through my dark silence, a great River of Life."[2]

CHAPTER 6

Preparing the Ground

A farmer went out to his field to sow grain....
Some of it fell on shallow soil with rock beneath....
Other seed landed in thistle patches, and the
young grain stalks were soon choked out. Still
other fell on fertile soil...and produced a crop
one hundred times as large as he had planted.

LUKE 8:5-8

Growing up at Willbrook, I learned much about the cultivation of crops. Daddy, who had a great love for the land, made sure of that. For example, I knew that before spring planting, the fields had to be prepared—rocks, weeds, and old roots removed, the soil "worked" to receive the seed. I love to see a freshly plowed field. I knew, too, that Clara's Uncle Straker would be supervising the workers, instructing them as to how to spot potential troublemakers in the gardens and uproot them before they damaged the crops.

A mentor is a gardener who helps to prepare the ground for the new things God is planting in His people. She is God's sharpened tool for digging up old roots of fear or resentment, for plowing up the soil of a woman's sensitive spirit, and for nourishing tender new growth.

She is divinely equipped to recognize your potential and to see where you fit. Her discernment about you will come from the following sources.

The Word of God

"Whom will he teach knowledge? And whom will he make to understand the message?... For precept must be upon precept, line upon line" (Isa. 28:9,10 NKJV). Everything your mentor says must line up with God's unchangeable Word. That puts a responsibility on the mentoree. As Eliza says, look it up for yourself and check it out.

> For the word of God is living and powerful, and sharper than any two-edged sword, piercing even to the division of soul and spirit...and is a discerner of the thoughts and intents of the heart.
>
> Hebrews 4:12 NKJV

Revelation Knowledge

The Greek word for revelation, *apocalypse,* is "to take the cover off, to expose." In other words, the light is on and you can see from the inside out! In the book of Revelation, God "takes the cover off" His Son through the apostle John: "I am the Alpha and Omega, the Beginning and the End," Jesus tells us (Rev. 1:8 NKJV). In other words, "I started it and I'm going to wrap it up!"

Wisdom and Experience

Your mentor will usually be a seasoned woman, but her wisdom is gleaned from God, not from experience alone. "If you want to know what God wants you to do, ask him, and he will gladly tell you, for he is always ready to give a bountiful supply of wisdom to all who ask him" (James 1:5).

When these three elements come into alignment, you can trust the person who is speaking into your life. Those who speak for God must know Him intimately. They will almost be able to read His mind, because they truly have His mind. (1 Cor. 2:16.) They will most certainly be equipped, through divine inspiration, to spot the roots and weeds that will impede your blossoming into full maturity.

Pulling Weeds

Along with the crops on our farm, our family has produced several generations of fine gardeners. Grandmother Williams planted magnificent camellias in her formal gardens in South Carolina. Again, however, it was Clara who taught me most about flowers. An uneducated botanist, she had her own greenhouse and grew fields of flowers behind the house—row upon row of zinnias and nasturtiums, marigolds and gladiolas. These she cut by the armload to bring to us through the summer months.

She also taught me that weeds do a fair imitation of flowers. Like the darnel, a biblical weed that is almost indistinguishable from wheat until it ripens at harvest (Matt. 13:24-30), such plants as Queen Anne's lace, daisies, thistles, and morning glory vines masquerade as lovely blossoms, but will choke out a farmer's cash crop if left unattended. Weeds multiply at a rate faster than any other living thing. Therefore, it is imperative that the serious gardener pull them up or learn to treat them with sprays.

Gossip is one such weed in your spiritual garden. The minute a tale is told, it can spread like wildfire and quickly rage out of control through the community grapevine. "Little white lies" also wear a disguise of innocence but will populate exponentially until there is an intricate network of deceit.

Mentors, with their wisdom and objectivity, can help you weed your garden. They will advise you to stop gossip in its tracks by being the last one to hear the story, thus breaking the cycle. They can help you stay alert as to which illegitimate flower is invading your fields and teach you to pull it up before it does any damage.

Aphids, Ants, and Other Pests

"I can't leave town without the aphids eating my roses!" I've heard John complain many times. My husband is an excellent gardener and knows that beautiful flowers require constancy. If he isn't close by to water, weed, and spray, the pesky creatures will chew away at his prize roses.

In the seasons and cycles of nature, God teaches us about the need to be nurtured. It is He who plants the seed of destiny within each spirit; but to encourage its growth, He often sends mentors. Like good gardeners, these women will stand by to watch for trouble spots in your life and to suggest methods of treating them. Some of your mentors may even be present when you are in full bloom, ready to release your fragrance and realize your purpose.

If you are not careful, though, the annoying "bugs" of stress and distraction will eat you alive. They will nibble at the edges of your time with the Lord. They will weigh you down with the cares of the world. Some bugs, like deep-seated sin, will burrow underground until they are in position to attack the root. Here they will hide, eating at the core of you until you miss the blooming season altogether.

Rooting Out Evil

With the purchase of my first small house from its occupants of forty-five years, I inherited a mature garden—boxwoods, dogwoods, camellias, roses—and lots of lovely, stately old trees. One of those trees had been cut just before we moved in, and the stump had not yet been removed.

When I found that the estimate for its removal matched our budget for an entire month, I proceeded to tackle the job myself. While the children napped, I got out a shovel and hoe and began to attack that stump. It was I who was soon stumped. I had not dug long before I realized that the root system spread out in a wide radius and that the taproot must go all the way to China. Nevertheless, all 5'2" and 120 pounds of me was determined to succeed.

I continued to hack away, hoping to break through the tangled growth but getting nowhere. It appeared to some of our neighbors that our front yard was the site for a new swimming pool! My husband suggested that I just cover the stump as best I could and plant around the base of the dead tree. I wasn't satisfied to take the easy way out and leave the thing rotting in the ground. Day after day, when the girls went down for their nap, I couldn't wait to get back outside to my self-imposed task, all to no avail.

Finally, I gave up and called in some of the men from my parents' farm. When Morgan and Jim couldn't make any headway with axes, they finally pulled their truck up to the now sizeable hole, positioned heavy chains around the stump, and gunned the engine. When the taproot gave way at last, there was a great tearing and wrenching as the earth released its hold.

That is the picture of deeply entrenched sin in a life. Dead places produce no fruit, no leaves, and no growth. It is necessary to identify and uproot the sin—stop doing it—in order to allow healing to take place.

Some sin—anger, lack of forgiveness, adultery, and various kinds of addiction—is buried so deep and remains for so long that you don't have the spiritual strength to uproot it by yourself. You need a "tree surgeon," someone skilled in the area of root removal.

Such people may come in the form of mentors familiar with biblical techniques of spiritual warfare and deliverance. In my case, God brought a river of women who imparted much to me as I grew and matured in Him.

My Favorite Root-Diggers
Uprooted, but Still Blooming

One early root-digger made me aware of wholeness and balance. Because I love beauty, graciousness, and refinement, God sent an elegant, cultured woman to guide me into new truth. We met at a conference, and our friendship blossomed instantly. Her impartation to me was to bloom where I was planted, with my branches stretching toward the Son.

We cannot help the circumstances of our birth—whether highborn or low—but we can allow God to use them to advance His purposes. Through this woman's wise counsel, I began to look around me to grasp the possibilities within my environment. As a result, I have never forgotten nor forsaken my small-town roots.

Thorns and Thistles

Another root-digger modeled spiritual etiquette in the workplace and taught me how to manage my time, leaving room for divine appointments. This Proverbs 31 woman advised me to plow my field, ridding it of some people and activities that hindered my spiritual growth, and to use greater discernment in scheduling projects and hiring helpers.

Bitter Roots

Several powerful women spoke prophetically into my life during one season, preparing me to receive the news of my sister's impending death, followed several years later by the death of my beloved father. This could have been a time when doubt and fear slipped in to choke out my faith, but these women had heard from the Lord, passed on His benediction of peace, and reminded me that nothing could separate me from His love and that I was not to take my eyes off Him! They continued the process of pruning and purifying in me, escorting me to the next level with the Lord.

Rooted in the Word

Still another root-digger stirred up the soil of my spirit and planted a deep desire to participate in Bible study and fellowship with other believers. I learned that God's Word "is right and good...is my only hope...is strength in all my troubles...refreshes and revives me...is my source of joy and singing...is my delight...stands firm in heaven...restores my joy and health...makes me wiser than my teachers...is a flashlight to light the path ahead of me and keep me from stumbling...is my joyous treasure forever" (excerpted from Ps. 119:39, 43, 50, 54, 77, 89, 93, 99, 105, 111).

A great bonus was in sharing our experiences as individuals within the group heard from the Lord through His Word. This discipline has remained consistent throughout my life, as I have participated in at least four Bible study groups.

The Taproot of Excellence

God's sense of humor showed up once again when a design client of mine rooted out an incorrect perception of bed making, of all things! I had always felt I knew how to make a bed properly—in fact, I had learned from Clara when I was just a child. But for some reason, the finer points of the procedure had eluded me until this incident. It seems you begin with a fitted sheet, add the first top sheet, layer with a light blanket, and finish off with a second top sheet before adding the bedspread.

From this, I learned that when one takes the time to learn the proper way of doing a thing, a much higher level of satisfaction is produced. This applies equally to spiritual matters. Every time I see a bed that is sloppily made, I recall this root-digger, who helped instill a love for excellence in all of life—a taproot that needs to remain—and plucked up a weed of mediocrity before it could mushroom into a destructive force.

Sowing Good Seed

Yet another, gifted with the ability to draw many to her through her genuine love and caring, went ahead of me, scouted out my field, worked its soil—sifting and cultivating—then sowed her own world of friends into it. It should come as no surprise, then, that these women were a choice crop, carefully tended, hand-picked, and presented to me as a gift. Each came with her own personality, talents, and gifts; I felt that I had known each one all my life.

I love the potpourri of these friendships with their rainbow of color, their heavenly blend of aromas. They are Broadway playwrights, Hollywood producers, actresses, writers, literary agents, designers, pastors, teachers, prophetesses, and businesswomen. They bring grace, a gentle spirit, patience, self-control, admonition, laughter, nurture, music, and great words of wisdom. They are God's women on assignment.

Fertile Soil

Over the next few years, I gave these powerful women of God permission to dig in my garden. They taught me about taking myself too seriously, about looking at the big picture. They encouraged me to be bold in the Lord, to become skilled in listening to God and in hearing my own heart. And they prophesied a new work.

Watch for the women God will send your way. Some, like Eliza, will walk softly, caressing your spirit like a spring breeze through the tulips. Others, like other friends and mentors I have known, will invade your inner sanctuary, armed with spiritual rakes and hoes and the strong Word of God, ready to do battle with ugly dead roots and withered stalks.

CHAPTER 7

Sowing in Love

"As You sent Me into the world, I have also sent them into the world...that the world may know that You have sent Me, and have loved them as you have loved Me."

JOHN 17:18,23

Do you remember that old *Peanuts* cartoon caption "Happiness Is..."? The creator, Charles Schulz, would sketch Charlie Brown interacting with his friends in some imaginary situation, and then proceed to outline everything happiness is from a delightfully childlike point of view.

The same scenario can be played out with "Love Is...." This time it is God's Word, not Charles Schulz's *Peanuts*, that defines the greatest emotion human beings are capable of knowing. Among other things, according to 1 Corinthians 13:

- "Love is very patient and kind" (v. 4).

- Love is "never boastful or proud" (v. 4).

- Love is "never haughty or selfish or rude" (v. 5).

And, of course, love is God. (1 John 4:8.)

Guided by the Holy Spirit, mentors, too, are extensions of God's love, sent to provide a safe place of true discovery. The mystery of you is hidden deep within. Love is the key that unlocks that mystery and steers you along the pathway of your destiny. *When you connect with a mentor, you are ready to experience revelation.* Your borders are enlarged, and you are stretched to receive even more truth about yourself, about God, and about the plan He designed for you before the foundations of the world.

First Corinthians 12 lists nine gifts of the Spirit (translated from the Greek word *charismata)* or "enablements."[1] According to Dr. Pat Robertson, author, television host, and founder of CBN, this phenomenon might be described as "a house wired for 200 amps of electricity, which could run an iron, a stove, a hot water heater, a woodworking shop, and any number of other electrical appliances. They all draw from the same power source. In the believer, the Holy Spirit is the source of power, and he can manifest Himself in healing, miracles, revelations, or utterances."[2]

A loving mentor will assist you in many ways, but it is in the area of cultivating your spiritual gifts that she will do some of her best work.

The Gift of a Word of Wisdom

Real wisdom is far more than learning how to succeed in business or life. That's worldly wisdom, and it can take you in the wrong direction. It is more than good advice or pretty proverbs stitched on fine linen and framed for your guest room wall. "The fear of the Lord is the beginning of wisdom" (Prov. 9:10 NKJV).

There is a distinct difference between worldly wisdom, the deep well of wisdom given by God, and the word of wisdom spoken by someone such as a mentor at a given moment in time. Dr. Robertson defines *word of wisdom* as "knowing about the future or having supernatural wisdom regarding a present situation" (see Luke 12:11,12 and Acts 6:8-10).[3]

The voice of the mentor is different from other voices. *When a wise woman hears from God and imparts that pure truth to you, it will be more powerful than anything you have heard before.* The words will sound richer, fuller, and more personal. They will cut through the fog like a laser beam of light piercing the darkness. You will hear differently as your spirit is quickened to receive the message targeted to you by the Holy Spirit. You will know that your mentor is speaking from a depth of knowledge that only God could have revealed to her. If you are wise yourself, you will soak it up like a sponge!

I have been astonished so many times at the way in which one of my mentors will nail an exact need or pending decision with a Scripture reference or seemingly offhand observation. This is not idle chitchat, but a hotline from heaven. When Eliza and some of the other mentors you will meet in this book speak, I know that their spirits are linked with mine in supernatural ways and that it is important to listen. It's almost as if my spirit is a huge catcher's mitt and I grab and hold on to the words of wisdom they impart to my heart.

The Gift of a Word of Knowledge

The word of knowledge is a gift of the Spirit—"discerning something that is not available to the senses"[4] and is often given as empowerment or even as a warning.

I once had a word of knowledge for a rebellious teenager. The fact that I was hardly a credible mentor at a time when my oldest daughter was in rebellion didn't seem to matter to God. This teenager's mother had called with a heart-wrenching plea to meet with her. She had been fasting and praying for the child. "Each time I pray," she said, "I see your face." Obviously, whether I was willing or not, God had chosen me for the assignment.

Impatient to have the whole thing behind me, and confident that I would be of no help to them, I told the mother to bring her daughter over on Saturday morning, "And don't go far," I said. "This will be a quick work."

In the first place, I knew the daughter didn't like me and was surprised that she had agreed to show up at all. I suspected this might be a complete waste of her time and mine. When she arrived, I led her into the living room, sent the mother on her way, and got right down to business without so much as saying hello.

"Let's pray," I began. "Father, give us revelation knowledge. Use this time for Your glory." The prayer was brief and to the point.

When I opened my eyes, I looked into her blank young face. "The Lord is showing me that you need to get everything straightened out in your life. There is a dynamic, powerful man in your future—not the one you're dating now (I suspected that she was seeing the high school football star)—a man with such a strong anointing that people are healed in his shadow. In fact, I can almost see his face. There are people gathered around him, and there is a beautiful holiness of the Lord present." I was as wide-eyed as she was at the information that was pouring out of me, the reluctant mentor that I was. "You need to hurry up to be ready," I told her.

Apparently she heeded the warning, because two years later she went to Mexico on a missions trip with our church and met her future husband! The young man "with such a strong anointing" whom I had mentioned in my word of knowledge was engaged in a ministry to children abandoned at the garbage dump. Strangely, this young woman had picked up Spanish as a second language and was prepared for what God was calling her to do. Today they are serving the Lord together, and each time I see her, we both know that it was God—not Ann Platz—who spoke to her that day.

The Gift of Faith

"Faith is the substance of things hoped for, the evidence of things not seen" (Heb. 11:1 NKJV). *The Living Bible* paraphrases these words in this way: "What is faith? It is the confident assurance that something we want is going to happen. It is the certainty that what we hope for is waiting for us, even though we cannot see it up ahead." What a gift!

A godly mentor is invaluable in stirring up the gift of faith when you are tempted to doubt. In fact, *a mentoring scenario fosters faith because you are building a relationship in the flesh with someone you are learning to trust, thus mirroring your relationship with God.*

When Peter stepped out of the boat one dark and stormy night and walked on water, he was responding to a Man he had come to love and trust. What he was doing at that moment was not logical, but love compelled him. It was only when Peter glanced around at the tossing waves and realized where he was that his faith faltered and he became fearful. (Matt. 14:33.)

If you don't keep your eyes fixed on Jesus, you'll sink! The absence of faith is fear. Mentors will teach you how to discern the voice of the Lord, telling you it's time to step out, and will then counsel you to keep your focus on Him, no matter what the circumstances around you.

I'll never forget the time I discovered my life verse, Joshua 1:9 (NKJV): "Have I not commanded you? Be strong and of good courage; do not be afraid, nor be dismayed, for the Lord your God is with you wherever you go." The Lord, who keeps His promises, has pledged to escort me "wherever I go"; and with my busy schedule, that's a full-time job. He is my bodyguard, protector, and defender. There is no place for fear when He is near. I keep this verse, beautifully framed, on the countertop in my bathroom to remind me of His constant provision.

A friend told me that this verse has changed her life. Unlike me, the "steel magnolia," she was more of a "clinging vine." That is, until the day she, too, discovered Joshua 1. Since then she has gone from wimp to warrior and has mentored many who have also learned to live by this promise.

The Gifts of Healing

The mentoring relationship is, first and foremost, a healing relationship. One cannot become a mentor until she herself is healed—at least emotionally and spiritually. Although a woman may be positioned to be an instrument of healing, she is not the healer. All healing comes from the Lord.

Not long ago, John and I had the pleasure of being in New York City with a well-known couple in ministry when John's old football injury acted up. At the slightest turn, his knee throbbed painfully, and he'd brought along a cane in anticipation of needing it before our trip was over.

We were having a late lunch in a Manhattan restaurant when John asked the man to pray for his knee. Right there, with staff and diners looking on, our friend knelt and prayed. The Lord healed John, and the pain immediately left. "My knee is feeling great!" John told me a little later, after the couple had left to go home. "There isn't a thing wrong with it!"

I, too, have received healing miracles. I *am* one! During the breakup of my first marriage, I was troubled with paralyzing panic attacks. Fear gripped my heart. The enemy often comes after the mind of a prophetic person, although at that time I had no idea that this was my gifting. As I allowed the Holy Spirit to mentor me, saturating my mind with God's Word and speaking the strong name of Jesus, the attacks subsided. Today, I can declare with certainty that I have been totally healed. This healing was not instantaneous like John's, but just as real and just as permanent.

Jesus spent most of His ministry healing people. From the blind man of Bethsaida, whose sight was restored after Jesus anointed him with a salve of mud and spittle (Mark 8:22-26), to the woman with the issue of blood, who received her healing by touching the hem of His robe as He was passing by (Mark 5:24-34), Jesus demonstrated His power as the healer. And He continues to heal. He does it His way and on His timetable. Still, He often chooses to use ordinary people as His partners, His vessels; ordinary elements—mud, spittle, oil—as the vehicles of healing. Nothing and no one can be discounted or discredited.

The Gift of Miracles

Webster defines a miracle as "an extraordinary event manifesting divine intervention in human affairs."[5] Miracles include such phenomena as stilling storms, restoring limbs, and resurrecting the dead. When one such extraordinary event takes place, we clearly know it's not anything a mere mortal could do but the very breath of God breathing life and power into human flesh.

Just because we do not routinely see such signs in this country does not mean that they do not exist in our day. Increasingly, I believe that we in the United States will experience these wonders before our very eyes just as believers in remote parts of the world have reported for decades now.

For example, I have heard of two "resurrections" in the past year or two—one, a confirmed medical miracle; the other, still under investigation. A man from a suburb of Nashville, Tennessee, suffered a heart attack and was pronounced clinically dead by the doctors. In his own words: "I felt myself leaving my body…no bright lights…no tunnels…no fancy stuff…I just left. The actual act of dying was so painless, so quick, and so without fear—just peace and release. I equate it to simply walking from one room to another. I became aware of being in a dark room, but not spiritually dark. In fact, I actually felt quite safe and peaceful. *A gate* led out of the room…although I never went through it to the other side.

"Suddenly, with every sense heightened, I perceived the presence of God…an enormous love that felt larger than the world, tangible love that flowed over me like warm honey…quickly followed by a sense of his holiness and righteousness, not frightening but marvelous and comforting. My heart knew in an instant that I could perceive only a portion of his perfection and it was simply dumbfounding. Brilliance beyond brilliance. Unmeasured intellect. Perfect love. In the presence of God, all I could do was worship."

When Jim regained consciousness soon after this divine encounter, everything changed. His whole perspective on the meaning of life took on new meaning, and he never misses an opportunity to share what God has done for him wherever he goes.

Another reported "death" occurred while a woman was having lunch with her husband at a well-known restaurant in an adjoining

OWING IN LOVE

suburb. Without warning, she fell forward, crashed into the counter, and thudded to the floor. The whole place erupted into action. One waitress rushed to cradle the woman's head in her lap and searched for a pulse. There was none and no other sign of life. Another person called "911." But one young waitress felt led to pray *in tongues, aloud,* over the woman's lifeless body! As she prayed, the woman revived! God is at work—today! God gives the gift of miracles for a purpose. Jesus told us what that purpose is: "Don't believe me unless I do miracles of God. But if I do, believe them even if you don't believe me. Then you will become convinced that the Father is in me, and I in the Father" (John 10:37, 38).

Don't be afraid of the miraculous. "Jesus' disciples saw him do many other miracles besides the ones told about in this book, but these are recorded so that you will believe that he is the Messiah, the Son of God, and that believing in him you will have life" (John 20:30, 31). Jesus and the Father are one. And God is love. He loves you enough to demonstrate His power so your faith in Him will be full. This kind of love is a miracle.

The Gift of Prophecy

The gift of prophecy takes the nonbeliever into the realm of belief and brings the believer straight to the heart of God. We are commanded to desire this gift above all others. (1 Cor. 14:1.) *Seeing the hand of God revealed and knowing that you are in the flow of the Spirit refreshes you like nothing else.* It touches you at a level that no other form of ministry can.

Grace Kinser left a fabulous legacy. This magnificent woman, a person I greatly admired and esteemed, was in and out of my life for years, without my ever suspecting that she was truly a mentor sent from God. I knew her story. As a younger woman, she had longed to give to several kingdom enterprises; but as her husband was a bakery route salesman, the funds were unavailable. So she prayed for a business.

God blessed her so abundantly that she was ultimately able to give to Liberty University and went on to bless such ministries as Kay Arthur's Precept Ministries. We kept bumping into each other at teas and ladies' events; but somehow, although she invited me to call or contact her, I never did. I was too busy.

At the wedding of a mutual friend, she put her arms around me and said, "I would love for you to decorate my house, but I can't bear the paint fumes." I knew she was in delicate health, but was surprised to learn of her death only three or four months later.

The bigger surprise came, however, when John and I purchased Mrs. Kinser's last home. As I was moving some things in, I found a little card with a message engraved on it: It was "my" verse—Joshua 1:9! "Have I not commanded you? Be strong and of good courage; do not be afraid, nor be dismayed, for the Lord your God is with you wherever you go" (NKJV). This card—left behind as if Mrs. Kinser intended for me to find it—was like a love gift from the Lord and is now one of my most cherished possessions. There is a pang of regret each time I realize what blessings I missed by not having had the pleasure of Grace Kinser's company as a mentor.

The story came full circle, however, when I began to arrange my furnishings and add touches here and there, and suddenly realized that her prophetic last words to me were coming true. I was, indeed, decorating Grace Kinser's house!

The Gift of Discerning of Spirits

A gift that is growing more and more important in these days of darkness and light is the gift of discerning of spirits—"the ability to see the invisible world of human spirits, angels, and devils."[6] Since the Word warns: "For false Christs shall arise, and false prophets, and will do wonderful miracles, so that if it were possible, even God's chosen ones would be deceived" (Matt. 24:24), it is imperative that we guard ourselves against falling into error.

That's where a mentor comes in handy. She is usually older and wiser and better able to discern truth. Joyce Meyer has a wonderful word on discernment: "Some people think they have discernment when actually they are just suspicious. Suspicion comes out of a mind that is not renewed to the Word of God; discernment comes out of the renewed spirit.

"True spiritual discernment will provoke prayer, not gossip. If a genuine problem is being discerned by a genuine gift, it will follow the scriptural pattern for dealing with it, not fleshly ways that only spread and compound the problem."[7]

The Gift of Speaking in Tongues and Interpretations

Although historically controversial and probably the lesser of the gifts, this one is as biblically valid as any (1 Cor. 12:10) and is edifying both personally and corporately. Jesus instructed Peter to stay in Jerusalem until He sent the Holy Spirit. The manifestation of His arrival was in tongues of fire on the heads of those gathered in that Upper Room—and the ability to speak in other languages. (Acts 1:4.)

Speaking in tongues, a language taught by the Spirit, private and custom-designed, is pure prayer. It proceeds, without the hindrance of a selfish agenda, directly to the throne of God. We will probably never fully understand the significance of this gift here on earth, but as a mentor it is a joy to lead others in receiving it.

A dear friend in the design world struggled for years with a serious problem. John and I loved him and attempted to impart to him as the opportunity arose. One summer night he attended church with us. Later we learned that he had had been diagnosed with AIDS. He spoke of growing up in the church and knowing that "religion" was "real," but that the world had such a hold on his life that he had been unable to withstand temptation.

We had a moving service of music and worship. The beautiful old hymns reminded him of his childhood faith, and after the service John led him in receiving the baptism of the Holy Spirit. There was no visible sign of the experience, but he was confident that he had received the gift. "Don't worry. I believe you'll receive the gift of tongues on your way home," John assured him.

Sometime later that night, the phone rang. It was our friend, exclaiming excitedly, "I got it! I got it!" He had put the top down on his convertible and had indeed received his prayer language on the way home.

There was a moment of silence, then another eruption from the other end of the line. "I can't believe what I'm seeing!" His telephone, which had been unplugged for cleaning, was not hooked into the wall. He was speaking to us through thin air!

The sweet presence of the Spirit carried our dear friend through his last days, until he died about eighteen months later. How precious of the Lord to send His Spirit, the Comforter, to be with him and usher him home.

The Power of Love

I collect friends. It's one of my passions. It isn't difficult for me since I'm a people person and just naturally enjoy getting to know folks. Consequently, knowing them and loving them usually go hand in hand.

Love is a secret weapon that transcends language, both earthly and heavenly, brings healing and wholeness, performs miracles, and sees prophetically. Without love, none of the gifts of the Spirit is effective; you're only a legal document. With love, the gifts are almost unnecessary.

Charlotte, too, is a mentor of God's love. She basks in it, she reflects it, she models it. I first met this well-known writer and speaker, a former journalist for the *Atlanta Journal & Constitution,* when she was at the most broken place in her life. Funny how God sends me across the paths of people in need of help, and I end up being the recipient of the blessing!

We became instant friends over brunch. Each of us had the other's name on a file card as someone we needed to know. With our busy schedules, neither had taken time to make the connection. This time God took care of it for us.

Learning that we were both to be in Montgomery on the same weekend—she, to address the Christian Woman's Club; I, to complete the decorating of the Alabama governor's mansion—we traveled there together. After I had completed my work at the mansion, I was able to hear her speak. By Sunday I knew this woman well—and already loved her.

Therefore, when she called the next week to say, "I think I'm being divorced," I was livid and fiercely protective of my new friend. While she had been blessed in her profession, her personal life was in shambles. The house had sold, and her husband wanted to split the furniture. It seemed to make little difference to him that the decision had also torn her heart apart.

"John and I want to help you find your new home," I told her. It wasn't long before the three of us had located a lovely apartment, but Charlotte was too dejected to care. "The Lord wants you to be surrounded by beauty to help heal your wounded heart," I insisted, not taking no for an answer. "We'll get busy and put things in order."

Typical of Charlotte, she responded with her wit still intact, bringing out every chipped dish she owned. "I'm only a broken teacup," she said wistfully.

At that moment God gave me a prophetic word for her, and we were both amazed at the revelation knowledge that poured out of my mouth. "Not only is God going to restore your life," I began, wondering where it would go from here, "but your next husband is going to have all that you do not have now—houses, *plural,* filled with antiques, fine rugs, porcelains, paintings, silver..."

"Forget it!" she snapped back. "I am not interested in remarriage."

I squinted, lips pursed. "Your life is not over. It's just beginning."

Putting a home together is one of the most enjoyable things I do. Consequently, the day sped by as we tweaked and fluffed her nest. I could see the hand of God as we added the little touches that make a house a home; and when I left her, we had jumpstarted the process. Not only that, but as a designer, I am able to buy overruns at a considerable discount that I only use for widows and others in reduced circumstances. Charlotte, a woman of great refinement and exquisite taste, was more than grateful.

I had no idea whom I was investing in. In her present situation, Charlotte was an unlikely mentor. So she surprised me one day by calling to ask how she could pray for me, adding that she believed I would become a writer with "many books in you." I laughed in her face. "I know who I am," I retorted, "and I know who I am *not*. And I am *not* a writer. Why, I can't even spell!"

"Writers are storytellers, and you're a storyteller."

In the next few weeks, she continued to encourage me with such astonishing comments as "Only a writer would say that." When I took that thought to the Lord, I sighed. "Charlotte loves me so much that she just *wants* me to be a writer like she is. But You and I both know how ridiculous that is, don't we?" The divine silence was deafening.

Then one day she called. "Have you heard of the prayer of Jabez?"

It sounded familiar. I recalled that it was in the Old Testament, mixed in there with the wars and kings. At that time, 1985, no one had heard of Bruce Wilkinson's little book by that title.

Charlotte laughed. "It's a short, very powerful prayer in 1 Chronicles, and I would like to ask permission to pray it over your life." Whereupon, she proceeded to do just that: "'Oh, that You would bless [Ann] indeed, and enlarge [her] territory, that Your hand would be with [her], and that You would keep [her] from evil, that [she] may not cause pain'" (1 Chron. 4:10 NKJV).

Sixteen years later, I am writing my ninth book—and Charlotte is the wife of a wonderful widower: "the finest man in Savannah," some say. At the time she married him, he had three households filled with fine furnishings! How loving and faithful God is.

Charlotte is my beloved friend and mentor. She is witty, wise, cherished, protected—and restored. There is no end to our season; even death will only separate us temporarily. Love, like a mentor who sows good seed, is eternal.

CHAPTER 8

Growing in Godliness

The fruit of the Spirit is love, joy, peace, longsuffering,
kindness, goodness, faithfulness, gentleness, self control....
If we live in the Spirit, let us also walk in the Spirit.

GALATIANS 5:22,23,25 NKJV

Think back to those days—whether long ago and far away, or of more recent vintage—when you fell in love for the first time. Winter seemed like spring. Time stood still. You sang in the rain and laughed at adversity. Love has no rhyme or reason. Love has no season.

In much the same way, when the Holy Spirit woos you to draw nearer to the heart of God, the very atmosphere around you is changed. You will find yourself hungering and thirsting for more of Him, desiring to be in His presence continually. As your next mentor moves into position, the Lord will provide the ideal growing conditions for your spirit. It is something like a greenhouse. No matter the weather—sunshine or rain, clouds or clear skies, testing or triumph—you will be covered by His hand of protection.

Your mentor, who is able to give you her full attention with no one else to compete for her time, will be able to guide you in godliness. The "God-shaped vacuum" within you, mentioned in the writings of Pascal, cannot be filled with anything else: not travel or fine cars or elegant cuisine or alcohol or money or possessions. There is a sign in your spirit that reads, "Reserved for the Things God Has for Me." You won't be satisfied with anything less.

Once you have tasted spiritual delicacies, the things of the world will lose their appeal. They will be as flat and tasteless as the Hungarian goulash my mother tried while traveling abroad. "Oh, taste and see that the Lord is good" (Ps. 34:8 NKJV). Now that you are beginning to suspect what you've been missing, you will crave heavenly manna, not the old "goulash" of your former life.

"Therefore, if anyone is in Christ, he is a new creation; old things have passed away; behold, all things have become new" (2 Cor. 5:17 NKJV). Even your "taste buds" will change!

A Heart After God

One who hungered for God was at the time a no-name shepherd boy, singing songs to the sheep on the Judean hillside. Alone for long hours with time on his hands, David communed with the Lord, composing melodies and lyrics in praise of his God. These songs, which have been recorded in the Psalms and make up the hymnal of the ancient Israelites, speak of sin and redemption, of loneliness and fulfillment, of fear and faith, of growth in godliness, of a kingdom lost and a kingdom found.

Who taught David how to write such music? In his case it was not a human mentor, but the Spirit of God moving in his heart and across the strings of his harp. His music soothed the tormented soul of King Saul and stormed the gates of heaven like a prayer.

When I think of David, I never think of him first as the greatest king of Israel. Neither do I label him as one of history's greatest sinners. (See the story of David's adulterous affair with Bathsheba in 2 Samuel 11.) I don't think first about David the giant-killer, the young warrior who fought and won great battles. No, I think of that shepherd boy, the one of whom God said, "David (son of Jesse) is a man after my own heart, because he will obey me" (Acts 13:22). David did a lot of growing on those hillsides because he was first listening. David, a man of humility, was always open to God's next move in his life.

Interesting, too, is the fact that David was not a *real* king. That is, he did not descend from a royal line in the natural. When Saul dropped the ball as leader of the Israelites, God looked for a man He could trust, one who would learn from His wisdom and counsel. That man was not Jonathan—Saul's son, the one most likely to succeed his father—but David. From a lowly shepherd of sheep, God called David up higher: "You shall shepherd My people Israel, and be ruler over Israel" (2 Sam. 5:2 NKJV). *God always calls us to a grander plan than the one we could have envisioned for ourselves.*

Through His covenant with David, God created a dynasty that would never end. "Of the increase of His government and peace there will be no end, upon the throne of David and over His kingdom, to order it and establish it with judgment and justice from that time forward, even forever" (Isa. 9:7 NKJV). Notice the capitalized pronoun in this verse. Suddenly we are talking about another King, the One who would come long after David to rule the whole world with "judgment and justice."

In reading the genealogy of this King, forty-two generations later, we see that He, Jesus, born of Mary, was "the Son of David, the Son of Abraham" (Matt. 1:1 NKJV).

What will be your legacy in forty-two generations, if the Lord tarries? Will you allow yourself to be mentored in godliness and to mentor others in order that the kingdom might increase?

God's Messenger

Another who eventually sought God with all his heart and allowed himself to be mentored was at first an unlikely candidate for sainthood. Paul's pedigree was impeccable. (Phil. 3:5,6.) After being thoroughly tutored in the Jewish law in synagogue school, he sat at the feet of Gamaliel, the leading rabbi of his day, and received today's equivalent of an Oxford education. In spite of all this "religious" training, Paul spent most of his time persecuting the true people of God. He stood by without intervening at Stephen's stoning (Acts 7:54-60) and harassed and slaughtered many Christians. The Lord finally had to interrupt a business trip to Damascus and strike Paul blind before he could "see" that he was headed in the opposite direction from where he had intended to go! (Acts 9:1-9.)

Following that dramatic encounter with the Lord, Paul cried out, "'What shall I do, Lord?' And the Lord told me, 'Get up and go into Damascus, and there you will be told what awaits you in the years ahead'" (Acts 22:10). For three days Paul fasted and prayed before God sent his first mentor, a godly man named Ananias, who gave him a prophetic word: "The God of our fathers has chosen you to know his will, and to see the Messiah and hear him speak. You are to take his message everywhere, telling what you have seen and heard" (vv. 14,15). Paul's "witness" was both preached and later printed in the form of half of the New Testament, including thirteen letters written to churches and individuals, thus "mentoring" every believer who has ever lived since that time!

When John and I counsel people who want to confess their grievous sins, we're not interested in hearing this kind of inverted "gossip." We simply point them to David and Paul and remind them that if God could forgive the sins of such men as these—after which He used them to proclaim His message to the ends of the earth—He can forgive and use them too!

Before a woman can grow in godliness, her heart must be right and her ear must be tuned to hear the Father's wisdom—either through a mentor or directly from His Word. As she grows up to be more like Him, the fruit of His Spirit will follow—"love, joy, peace, patience, kindness, goodness, faithfulness, gentleness and self-control" (Gal. 5:22,23).

Testing Time

If you have never been or are not now being tested, then you're still in the first grade. The Christian life is a series of exams. It is necessary to pass each one before you can move on to the next level with the Lord.

Spiritual tests are something like the competition an athlete experiences each time he or she enters a contest. *There is preparation to be made, a challenge to be met, encouragement from the stands, and a victory to be won.*

The Preparation

When a runner is preparing for a 10K race, a rigid list of training rules must be observed. Months before the event, the runner is daily working out, gradually building up muscle and stamina for the big day. Besides the actual practice runs, a strict diet must be followed.

The runner must know how many carbohydrates to ingest before the run, as fat is burned off at a steady rate.

Since the body is a well-crafted machine, each part is integral to every other part. Ultimately, every organ works together to produce the desired effect—strength and endurance to cross the finish line.

The Challenge

Each race or contest presents an opportunity to improve your overall standing. A runner is not just in the event to win over the competition, but to increase speed, build stamina, and better her own record.

So, too, is the race of life. The grueling discipline of preparation, the long hours of practice, the wind sprints and dashes—all come together in the actual moment of competition. At the end of the race, the winner will be the one who made the greatest investment ahead of time!

The Cheerleaders

In the stands or on the sidelines are those who have come to cheer the contestants on to victory. They shout encouragement, pull for their favorites, and applaud when the race is over.

The Holy Spirit provides that kind of encouragement through a "cloud of witnesses" who are looking on as we run.

Since we have such a huge crowd of [people] of faith watching us from the grandstands, let us strip off anything that slows us down or holds us back, and especially those sins that wrap themselves so tightly around our feet and trip us up; and let us run with patience the particular race that God

has set before us. Keep your eyes on Jesus, our leader and instructor [our Mentor].

Hebrews 12:1,2

Mentors are God's cheerleaders, the physical presence of heavenly witnesses. In partnership with the Holy Spirit, their primary purpose is "to awaken the mentoree to his or her uniqueness as a loved child of God, created in the image of God for intimacy of relationship that empowers the individual for authentic acts of ministry."[1] A mentor champions the mentoree on to victory, sometimes cheering from the stands, more often walking alongside to give encouragement and lend support on the long and difficult path to maturity.

The Victory

After the race is over, the winner receives the gold medal or an engraved trophy or a cash prize—her reward for diligence. There is wild applause as friends and family gather to celebrate.

While we will enjoy small victories on earth, the real crown will go to those who "have fought the good fight...have finished the course...have kept the faith" (2 Tim. 4:7 NKJV). The crown of righteousness will be given by the Lord, "the righteous Judge...on that Day" (v. 8 NKJV). Most victories, however, don't come easily. Along with skill and effort, they require courage and endurance.

A product of the Roaring Twenties, Gertrude Ederle was a thoroughly modern American girl who enjoyed jazz music and ahead-of-her-time challenges. She was only nineteen when she became the first woman to swim across the English Channel, braving the dangerous currents and cold temperatures to carve a place for herself in the annals of sports history.

Fourteen hours and thirty minutes after she stepped into the icy waters of the channel at Cape Gris-Nez, France, she emerged on an English beach, to the cheers of thousands who had burned bonfires to light her way.

An unknown writer once wrote:

> *When care is pressing you down a bit—*
> *Rest if you must, but don't you quit.*

What if Gertrude Ederle had not responded to the cheers of those crowds, like mentors who are standing in the wings to wave you on? What if she had balked at the icy water? What if she had stopped when the day faded to night? What if she had quit?

Second Wind

My husband, John, is not a quitter. His first wife, Marion, died of alcoholic hepatitis. Their long life together—thirty-four years—was marred by bouts of alcoholic dysfunction. She was not an easy woman to love. Even John's saintly mother encouraged him to divorce her and put an end to his misery. But John stood by her, praying for her to come to the Lord.

Husbands and wives are natural mentors. Each one brings to the marriage something the other lacks as the two become one. God planned it that way. If hearts are receptive, they can learn from one another, halve their troubles, and double their joy. Unfortunately, imperfect people often disrupt God's perfect plan.

When Marion's liver was gone, she willed herself to die. John admitted her to a hospital and continued to pray, hoping that it was not too late for a miracle, but she grew weaker by the day. She refused to budge, too, on the subject of her salvation. She hadn't given herself

to the Lord in life, and it appeared that she would stubbornly cling to her own way even in death.

Learning from the doctor and nurse that she didn't have much time left, John made a last appeal: "Marion, I think it's time you got right with the Lord. Soon you won't have any choice in the matter. It'll be heaven—if you choose Jesus—or it'll be hell for all eternity. Please let me pray the sinner's prayer with you. Just say the words after me."

At this point Marion was a living skeleton, with barely enough breath left to whisper. She gave a feeble nod of agreement. He began the age-old words of confession and repentance, relieved when she mumbled them after him. At the very end, she managed a little smile and said, "I'm sorry I didn't do it sooner."

He patted her knee, shocked to find that it was as hard as stone. The nurse, who was standing by, stepped nearer. "I didn't want to tell you, but rigor mortis started in her feet this morning."

What if John had not persevered all those years? What if he had failed to mentor well? What if, at the last, she had not listened and obeyed God's still, small voice—while there was still time? Yet John stayed the course. Now he has the satisfaction of knowing that his first wife is celebrating her last-minute victory, and he is blessed in this life with another family, excellent health, and a clear and peaceful conscience. Not only that, but wherever John travels in the world, he leaves behind a trail of conversions. Like the apostle who bears his name, John is an evangelist, another man after God's own heart.

Stretch Marks

I have a very clear picture of who I am before the Lord—and it is not a pretty sight. I look like someone who answered the door after just awakening from a nap without having taken time to adjust her makeup—hair sticking straight out, mascara-smeared eyes, no lipstick. I may be growing in godliness, but at any given moment you'll catch me in my "old" skin before the "facelift"!

I thank the Lord that He uses me in spite of my arrogance, my stupidity, and my unbelief. It is His mercy and grace on my life and His patience with me that produce the fruit. Better never trust yourself—or anyone else—too much, or you're heading for a fall. C. S. Lewis sounded a strong warning for mentors and mentorees when he wrote: "We must recognize the true Giver. It is madness not to. Because, if we do not, we shall be relying on human beings. And that is going to let us down. The best of them will make mistakes. All of them will die. We must be thankful to all the people who have helped us; we must honor them and love them. But never, never pin your whole faith on any human being: not even if he [or she] is the best and wisest in the whole world."[2]

That said, let me add that mentors are still part of God's recipe for growth, and growth involves painful stretching. He will allow the circumstances that require you to demonstrate the fruit of the Spirit, thus giving you a good idea of how your garden grows. For most people, two difficult areas are forgiveness and obedience.

Forgiveness

This is simply a command—no opting out. Forgive, and you will be forgiven. (Matt. 6:12.) It's as simple as that. Forgiveness is basic to going deeper with God and growing up in Him. In fact, I would say that a lack of forgiveness fertilizes a root of bitterness, and is the main obstacle to spiritual growth. You really can't progress along the path of righteousness without it. You can justify all you want to, or play the

"just-look-what-he-did-to-me" game, but when it comes right down to it, God said it and we save a lot of time just doing it! And that leads me to the second difficulty: obedience.

Obedience

With our human nature being what it is in this fallen world, we are cursed with a fundamental rebellion when it comes to obeying authority. Some traditional wedding vows now omit the word *obey.* Defiant young people scorn the law and flaunt their "rights." Even schools, caught up in humanistic philosophy, have removed the "rod of correction" and surrendered to the modern permissive mentality. Could that be part of the reason we have such tragedies as the one in Columbine and other massacres in the classrooms of America?

God's Word is clear: "Has the Lord as great delight in burnt offerings and sacrifices, as in obeying the voice of the Lord? Behold, to obey is better than sacrifice" (1 Sam. 15:22 NKJV). I don't know about you, but if obedience means this much to the Lord, I think I will take it very seriously.

A friend recently shared a life experience that cuts to the heart of both of these stretching places. After years of an abusive marriage with resulting health problems, she had come to the end of herself. In her pain and confusion, she had developed a relationship with a woman who had joyfully agreed to mentor her in the deeper walk, and now she was seeking the Lord as never before. In fact, ill at the time, she was lying in bed praying that He would reveal Himself— when that's exactly what He did!

Hovering over the region of her heart was a warm "ball" of pure love. No visible Person appeared, but my friend knew that this was the presence of God. Overwhelmed by this unprecedented event, she listened as He delivered a surprising message. *Call your ex-husband and ask for his forgiveness.* What? Had she heard correctly? Surely the Lord understood that she had been the victim, not the perpetrator of the abuse. Yet the still, small voice persisted. *Call him.*

Feeling dizzy, weak, and a little ridiculous, she decided to act on this strange word. Besides, she reasoned, her ex-husband, who had married a businesswoman who traveled the world, would probably be in Tahiti or somewhere, and wouldn't even answer the phone—or so she hoped.

To her immense surprise, someone did answer on the first ring: his second wife! My friend had not expected this, but pressed bravely forward. If she didn't follow through now, she might back out and disobey the sure word from the Lord.

Although they were on their way out the door for an evening function, the ex-husband took the call. "I believe that two people make a marriage and two people break it," my friend told him. "I'm really sorry for anything I may have done to contribute to the failure of our marriage. I forgave you in my heart a long time ago, so now I'm only asking that *you* forgive *me*."

She had obviously taken him off guard, because she was greeted with a sputtered reply. "Well...uh...I believe this might take a little more time than I have at the moment...but sure...uh...I forgive you."

My friend dates the beginning of her emotional and physical healing to this telephone call. In obedience to the Lord, she was engaged in what some might call "mending fences."

Mended Fences

As a farmer's daughter, I know what happens when the gate is open and the fences are down. The cows get out and trample the corn!

In fact, everything that is inside gets out and everything that should stay outside invades the garden.

What happens in those unguarded moments when the fences are down? The predators take over: Thieves, weeds, and animals ruin the good groundwork that has been done. What is the root of this destruction? It could be fences rotted or rusted due to neglect, the erosion of time, or perhaps incorrectly laid foundation or posts.

That's why gates and gatekeepers are so important. Someone must stand guard over the valuable treasures inside, to be on the lookout for weak places and sound the alarm when something is amiss. Someone must teach and instruct and champion. Someone must nurture and fertilize the good growth that has begun in you.

In 1 Chronicles 9:22, we find that in the early days of Jerusalem there were 212 gatekeepers! These gatekeepers were assigned to the four corners of the city and were given specific instructions as to their duties in guarding the city gates. It was a trusted office, and each gatekeeper was responsible for a particular area of labor. Some "lodged all around the house of God because they...were in charge of opening it every morning" (v. 27 NKJV).

Your mentors will open the gate of your understanding and watch for the "little foxes" that may try to root under the fence or find a weak place in the structure. When a break occurs, the gatekeeper must make immediate repairs. Leaving the fence down or weakened invites trouble.

I remember the women who spoke prophetically at a time when I might have left the gate open. Instead, when Mother called from South Carolina to say, "Mary Ashley went to be with the Lord about five minutes ago," an unearthly calm descended over me. Here I was, hearing the dreaded news about my precious sister, thinking that this was not the way I had expected to feel when it happened. Those women of God had dug in my garden; they had uprooted bitterness and taught me about godly living; and, through their powerful, anointed prophecies, they had prepared me for this moment.

I was covered in God's grace and peace. Two friends at the airport, on their way to a horticulture convention, escorted me to the Delta gate. They had no idea that my sister had just died, and I didn't want to dampen their idle chatter with sad news. I had to smile to myself at the thought that my heavenly Father had provided such unlikely angels in this time of crisis.

Though thousands would pass by to offer their condolences in the next few days, I received everything I needed from the Lord's own hand. He enabled me to plan the funeral, making all the arrangements to decorate it in an elegant style befitting my sister—the Lady of the Flowers. I was absolutely stunned at the protection hovering over our entire family—from my father, the patriarch, to Mary Ashley's husband and two-year-old son. We were all walking under a canopy of grace.

Thanks to these mighty women of God, this episode in my life proved that I had done some growing in godliness. *There would be further tests and trials, but the harvest was proving to be rich and abundant—worth it all.* I could almost hear Clara singing the words of one of her old spirituals:

> I looked over Jordan, and what did I see,
>
> Coming for to carry me home?
>
> A band of angels coming after me,
>
> Coming for to carry me home.
>
> Swing low, sweet chariot
>
> Coming for to carry me home.[3]

CHAPTER 9

The Harvest

"The harvest truly is plentiful, but the laborers are few.
Therefore pray the Lord of the harvest to send out
laborers into His harvest."

MATTHEW 9:37,38

Harvest time—my favorite time of the year as a child growing up on a cotton plantation in South Carolina. Memories come in crowds. Pigtails swinging as I trot barefoot down a dusty road to watch the harvesters in the cool of the day. The smells of summer—a mingled perfume of earth and growing things and good, honest sweat. Great bales of cotton, plucked from the boll, now stacked on flatbed tractors to be hauled to market. The shouts of applause from the field hands gathered around as the scales register a record yield.

Before the farm became automated, Daddy slaughtered hogs at harvest time. He would put on an annual barbecue afterward at the house for those who had worked so hard and long and were now ready to enjoy the fruits of their labor.

What a picture of the mentoring season. The laborers (your mentors) have overseen the planting of the crop (your spiritual gifts), have nurtured and tended it, have guarded it against "boll weevils" and other intruders, and have watched it grow. *You have absorbed a little of the essence of each of your mentors that has enriched the soil of your life, and they will be the first to rejoice when you begin using your gifts to bless others.* When you wake up to the truth of the spiritual giftings God has placed in you, you will be ready for the increase!

The Awakening Heart

When I complained about the rain that interfered with my outdoor play one day, Daddy peered at me over his glasses, shook his head, and lamented, "It's hard for me to believe that you're a farmer's daughter." Although I didn't share my father's passion for the farm, I *was* intrigued with the awakening of the earth in the springtime, when the tiny seedlings would begin pushing through the clods of dirt, transforming the fields to a sea of tender green. By midsummer, those shoots would become—almost miraculously, it seemed—clouds of fluffy cotton. How anything that had started out to be one thing could somehow become something entirely different was a wonder to me.

It is that kind of miracle your mentor will assist in bringing forth when she recognizes who you are in Christ. You may look like a wife, a mother, a businesswoman, or a farmer's daughter, but until God shines His spotlight on your spirit, you may not be able to identify your true worth or your latent abilities. Sometimes it takes a more objective partner in the process to discover who you really are.

As you begin seeing the powerful gifts God has uniquely placed in you to produce a harvest for Him, you will be released to begin using those gifts more fully. Once the light is turned on, you will see differently and hear differently.

There is a language of love that God has written just for the two of you. Just as you and your husband, if you are married, may have a special song that immediately causes you to think about one another, sometimes the Lord will give you a song that is especially yours and His. Just hearing the melody will evoke tenderness toward the One who knows you best and loves you most.

One song that I would never reveal keeps turning up in places where I minister and serve. Sometimes, completely unexpectedly, it will be played in a meeting, and I will feel God's approval: *Well done, daughter. I am pleased with you.* This personal word from my Lord always brings tears to my eyes or a secret smile to my lips. It is "our" song.

Sometimes it is a verse of Scripture that He writes indelibly on your heart, key words and phrases that ring so true and pierce so deeply. One such verse for me, which I have shared before, is Joshua 1:9: "Be bold and strong!... For remember, the Lord your God is with you wherever you go." Your mentor will teach you to be looking and listening for this "new" language. It will strengthen and encourage you when no one else is around.

Lord of the Harvest

I cannot emphasize too often or too strongly that this book is not really about mentors and mentorees, about what we know or what we should learn, about how we teach or what we receive from our teachers. It is about Him. *He is the planter, the nurturer, and the Lord of the harvest.* And the harvest He is most interested in reaping is the harvest of your inner self, the person He loves and has equipped to use for His own purposes.

My friend Charlotte experienced a harvest of mammoth proportions. You have already met her in a previous chapter. She is the renowned writer and speaker whose world was shattered when her husband walked out. But just listen to the next installment of her story.

I met Charlotte at a time when there was nothing ripe on that fig tree—no growth, no hope, no fruit. She didn't want to hear that life was not over and that the best was yet to come—and certainly not from me! But I was determined to speak life into her, to deliver the word the Lord was unfolding. I stood my ground while she retreated, tearful in the midst of the pathetic pile of broken teacups she had assembled.

"I don't care how many things are broken in your life!" I told her. "I don't care if your husband has run off with half the family heirlooms! All these years you've sown good seed into people, the world-class writing you've done, the praying, the caring—you listen to me, Charlotte Hale, the harvest is coming, and you can't stop it!"

While she sat there like a knot on a log, I laid out the vision the Lord was showing me for Charlotte. I saw her future, unfurling like the petals of a rose: more worldly goods than she had ever had before, more opportunities to serve the Lord, more joy, more fulfillment, more love. "You'd better get up from there, because you have work to do. The Lord has so much for you!" I finished decorating her apartment, despite her lack of enthusiasm, and sailed off, sure that God would be true to His Word.

Several years later, I flew to Savannah to decorate my dear friend's new home—one of *three* belonging to her brand-new husband. As I inventoried Charlotte's "harvest," my emotions ran the gamut. *Oh, Lord, You are so faithful. Your Word is true! "If you give, you will get! Your gift will return to you in full and overflowing measure, pressed down, shaken together to make room for more, and running over"* (Luke 6:38).

Here before me was just a token of Charlotte's true treasures that are deposited to her account in heaven. It was the vision I had "seen" that day in her apartment: the priceless antiques, the rich Oriental rugs, the paintings, and the porcelains. Three times more than she had ever had before. So much that she was able to give her sister the furnishings from her former home out of the "overflow."

Although there was nothing I could see with my physical eyes that day in Charlotte's apartment, the Lord had revealed His plan for her through the eyes of the Spirit. He chose to use me—although it could have been anyone—to be a warrior mother mentor for her, to do spiritual warfare in her behalf. Soon afterward God picked Charlotte up, dusted her off, and sent her back out to do His will. The book deals began coming in, and she was about her Father's business again.

This is only one of many stories I could relate to you. Over and over again I have witnessed the provision of the Lord for His people. He's a good Daddy *(Abba)*. He never abandons His children. He is the Giver of every good and perfect gift. (James 1:17.) When the enemy comes in to ravage and destroy, the mentor is positioned to stand in the gap, to guard the gifts until they are ripe for the harvest.

Sowing and Reaping

If you were about to take a little break and lay this book aside, I'd recommend that you wait. If you thought you knew everything there is to know about the principle of sowing and reaping, I suggest that you read on. This may be the most important part of the entire chapter.

Remember that you can't ignore God and get away with it: a [woman] will always reap just the kind of crop [she] sows! If [she] sows to please [her] own wrong desires, [she] will be planting seeds of evil and [she] will surely reap a harvest of spiritual decay and death; but if [she] plants the good things of the Spirit, [she] will reap the everlasting life which the Holy Spirit gives [her]. And let us not get tired of doing what is right, for after a while we will reap a harvest of blessing if we don't get discouraged and give up.

Galatians 6:7-9

I had hoped to come up with some fresh, new words to superglue this truth in your mind, but how could I possibly improve on the clear Word of God? He means exactly what He says: *You reap what you sow.* It's as simple as that—and as profound. If you dream of being married to the wrong man, you may wake up in the middle of a nightmare. If you as a believer choose to do drugs and then you become addicted, you will go to heaven when you die, but you may have to endure the torture of withdrawal in a detox center here on earth. If you decide to bring up your children using the permissive approach and ignore God's instructions for parenting, be prepared to deal with rebellious, defiant teenagers down the road. If you plant corn, you get corn. If you plant poison, you reap poison—and contaminate the earth at the same time.

A mentor also does some sowing. She sows life and light into your spirit. She exposes the darkness, offers loving correction (sometimes loudly), imparts truth, and provides a safe haven for your soul. When you are in a dry place, she is a refreshing drink of water. When you can't hear or interpret the voice of God, she relays to you what He is saying. (Acts 8:29-39.) When you are lying on the side of the road, bloodied and beaten, she stops to offer emergency aid as only she is uniquely equipped to do. (Luke 10:30-37.) She is God's partner, working with Him to advance His kingdom agenda for your life.

Without the mentors in my life, I would not have seen where I belong in the big picture. It has nothing to do with personality, but where I fit in the body of Christ. *You, too, have a personal calling that was designed for you before the foundations of the world.* (Jer. 1:5.)

God knows what that is and sometimes shares the secret with hand-picked mentors who will spotlight your spiritual gifts. They will guide you to find your part of the puzzle and the way in which the Lord wants you to join your gifts with those of other people. It's the principle of multiplication.

Multiplication—God's Increase

The harvest is more than the yield of one season. Get out the family Christmas picture and take a look at your crop. A fairly recent photograph that Mother framed and mounted on a wall at home shows how widespread hers and Daddy's influence has become. In the photo, dressed all in red and green, hair combed and smiles sparkling, are nine grandchildren and eight adorable great-grandchildren. I can hear Daddy now, exclaiming over the large return on his investment. "I will multiply your descendants as the stars of heaven" (Ex. 32:13 NKJV) was not spoken to Abraham alone!

In speaking of the family, I want to mention the mentoring role of older women encouraging the younger "to love their husbands, to love their children, to be discreet, chaste, homemakers, good, obedient to their own husbands, that the word of God may not be blasphemed" (Titus 2:4,5 NKJV). With families so fractured and fragmented in our society and moral values less and less important to the general public, there is no question in my mind that this passage is the very heart of this book. The concept is so crucial that I believe we should take these verses apart and study each aspect of God's instruction.

Love Your Husbands

You married him, now how do you keep him? By following God's recipe for a happy marriage: "See to it that [you] deeply [respect your] husband—obeying, praising and honoring him" (Eph. 5:33). That means doing all the little things you know how to do to nurture, comfort, and encourage him.

Love Your Children

I have been shocked lately at the number of women who are not only abandoning their children, but actually murdering them (not to mention the continued high rate of abortion)! This is a society of throwaway children. We desperately need to hear God's Word on maintaining healthy, whole families. Love is the key.

Be Discreet

Webster defines this word as "having discernment or good judgment in conduct, especially in speech."[1] Apparently Paul is ruling out idle gossip and any kind of careless talk that would damage someone's reputation.

Be Chaste

Chastity is purity of thought and action. Every deed—whether good or evil—begins with a thought. Therefore, reining in the mind is the remedy for every kind of sin.

> The weapons of our warfare are not carnal but mighty in God for pulling down strongholds, casting down arguments and every high thing that exalts itself against the knowledge of God, bringing every thought into captivity to the obedience of Christ.
>
> 2 Corinthians 10:4,5 NKJV

Be a Homemaker

I love the version that translates this word as "keepers at home" (v. 5 KJV). Stay-at-home moms and women who opt not to work outside the home, be encouraged! God does not only value your skills, but He considers this role your primary calling. You are the ones who "keep" the home together and working properly, guard its precious treasure, and extend the doors of hospitality to others. Women who also work outside the home to care for their families deserve support and encouragement as well.

Be Good

This word has so many definitions in the English language that it has all but lost its meaning. Only God is truly good. (Luke 18:19.) His Word mirrors His reflection. As we pore over it and wash ourselves in the healing words, we become more like Him.

Be Obedient to Your Own Husband

Oops! "Now you've gone to meddling," as southern grandmothers might say. If we can just remember that Jesus is our husband and that he has ordered the hierarchy of the home, then it is easy to accept the chain of command He has established. Obedience is not a nasty word. It simply means coming under the authority and *protection* of another.

Eliza has a word for young women who desire a ministry. If they are married and have children, she says: "Go home and take care of your family. That is your ministry." There will be plenty of time later to follow the Lord into other paths of service. But for now—and these years will fly by, believe it or not—*you will be reproducing yourself as you sow good seed into your children.* Teach them to love the Lord, to follow His laws for living, and to tell others about Him. In so doing, one day you will be able to say, as you survey your family portrait: "I have no greater joy than to hear that my children walk in truth" (3 John 4 NKJV).

Multiplication, of course, applies to much more than mere physical reproduction. When you blow on a dandelion, the tiny little seeds travel with the wind, and you never know where those seeds are going. Through your mentors, God blows His breath on your gifts and disperses them to the uttermost parts of the earth. As you use your gifts, the gifts increase. The increase comes exponentially as the first person you touch impacts another, the next shares with someone else, and the ripples continue all the way across the nations. How precious of God that some of your first mentorees are your very own children whose lives will help to transform the world.

Reaping the Reward

After you have been enlightened about your gifts, you'd better not hide them under a bushel. (Mark 4:20-22.) You will want to act on that which has been imparted to you. If not, you may become ingrown and rot on the vine. Where God had rich rewards and glorious plans for you, He may even pass you by and call someone else to take your place. Reinhard Bonnke testifies that he knows he was not God's first choice to be a worldwide evangelist, but the other two said no! Now he has a global ministry, with millions of people responding to the call to salvation and miracles occurring regularly in his huge crusades.

Moses raised all kinds of objections when God called him to lead the children of Israel out of Egypt. For every instruction God gave, Moses retorted with a "but." *"But* I'm not the person for a job like that," he whined (Ex. 3:11). *"But*...if I go to the people of Israel and tell them that their fathers' God has sent me, they will ask, 'Which God are you talking about?'" (v. 13). *But* "they won't believe me..." (4:1). *But* "I'm just not a good speaker. I never have been, and I'm not now...I have a speech impediment" (v. 10). Each time God countered with a promise to supply everything needed, and finally He called Moses' brother Aaron to mentor him. The harvest they produced brought an entire nation out of bondage.

When God calls, either directly or through a mentor, don't say no. If you do, you'll miss the greatest blessings of your life!

I shudder to think that I almost said no once. By now you know a great deal about my relationship with Charlotte. There is more. I've told you that she prayed the prayer of Jabez over me—and she has continued to do so for eighteen years. You know that she believed I would write and speak—gifts I never dreamed resided within me. She even hinted at a ministry "to the nations." In fact, I scoffed when she told me that.

Each time we were together, however, she continued to nudge me in that direction, and I found myself involved in some book projects that could have only come from God's heart. The book you are reading is my ninth, and the others are now distributed all over the world. I decided that this kind of worldwide distribution was what Charlotte had meant by her insinuation that I would be ministering "to the nations." In fact, I hoped it was. The idea of traveling to Africa or Afghanistan scared me, but the Lord had another idea.

The moment I stepped on a television stage, I got it. The prayer of Jabez that Charlotte has prayed for me is being answered even as you read these words. My "borders" are being "enlarged." Through mentors, the Lord has led me to a network of people and resources. A foundation is being laid for multiple programming and a syndicated radio show that will impact people of every background, social level, religious belief, and culture. If I had said no to my first mass-media opportunity, I would still be an interior designer, merely decorating people's homes instead of their hearts.

Called To Celebrate

As I have grown in my walk with the Lord, the harvest celebrations of my childhood have taken on new meaning. I have come into an understanding of the Jewish feast days, still practiced by most observant Jews and many Christians who love Israel and their Jewish roots.

One of the seven festivals God has decreed that His people observe is the Feast of Tabernacles, or *Sukkoth*. This was the time of the final ingathering of the harvest, anticipating the immense harvest of souls prior to Jesus' *(Yeshua's)* return. Through this annual feast, the people of God were made aware of their years of wandering and of the temporary nature of their earthly housing as, for eight days each year, the faithful dwell in a *Sukkoth* (booth).[2] The apostle John tells us that Jesus "dwelt among us" (John 1:14 KJV). Our dwelling is also temporary. The greatest "housing"—many mansions—lies ahead!" (John 14:3.)

Several years ago, John and I, feeling such a connection with our Jewish "kinfolks," had the great pleasure of being in the Holy Land at the time of the Feast of Tabernacles. Thousands of people, including American tourists like us, thronged the cities to celebrate this joyous festival with music and dance. Flatbed trucks like the ones on my father's farm were heaped with produce, the first fruits of the land. The cotton crops, nurtured by an elaborate system of irrigation engineered by great Israeli minds, had yielded four times the abundance of our own in the United States. Huge baskets of fruit displayed strawberries as large as tomatoes, and specimen oranges, grapefruit, and lemons that are exported to other, more tropical countries in record numbers! Truly we were seeing Isaiah's prophecy fulfilled: "Israel shall blossom and bud, and fill the face of the world with fruit" (Isa. 27:6 NKJV) and "the desert will blossom with flowers. Yes, there will be an abundance of flowers and singing and joy!" (Isa. 35:1,2).

The procession of truckloads and wagons filled with magnificent produce and flowers rivaled anything we had ever seen, even in the Rose Bowl Parade on New Year's Day. What a picture of the fullness and bounty of God released to bless His people.

One memory stands out in my mind as a sweet touch from the Lord. As the animals, groomed for the occasion, passed by, I noticed that even the cows were garlanded with roses! When we returned from our trip to share our experience with my parents, Daddy winked. "So now you're suggesting that we put roses on our cows?"

Daddy would be proud of his citified daughter. He was a good mentor for that season, and I learned much from him about the importance of sowing good seed and the cycle of nature, but I also learned deeper values about the soil of the spirit and reaping the harvest.

I know my heavenly Father is also pleased when I use my gifts to extend His kingdom and to bless others. At times, when "our" song is playing and I am hearing His heartbeat, I even sense that He is giving me a divine wink and a little shove. "Go enjoy the party! Enter into the joy of your Lord." (Matt. 25:21.)

CHAPTER 10

Guarding Your Gifts

"I have set watchmen on your walls....
"Go through the gates! Prepare the way for the people."

ISAIAH 62:6,10

I love the idea of guardians, those who are entrusted with material things—or persons—of great value. Only those of sterling character can be appointed to this position. Guardians are respected and esteemed people of integrity. They might also be called shepherds or custodians of that which is of infinite worth. And then, of course, there are guardian *angels*. I know I have met some of them in my lifetime. One or two "angelic types" have mentored me!

You and your spiritual gifts are among the most precious things God has created. Because He prizes you so highly, He has sent guardians (mentors) to intersect your path from time to time. Just as an underage, orphaned child must be placed in the custody of some older, wiser person, so you, as a woman who is growing in godliness, need someone who has been down that path before you. You need someone whom the Lord trusts to look out for your interests, to guard the gifts and potential deposited in you.

It's not a selfish thing at all. It is a matter of spiritual economy. God wants to guard your gifts so that there will be abundance for His people. As you use your gifts, others will be blessed—even if you feel that you have nothing to give.

The delightful pastor Dr. E. V. Hill was once interviewed on TBN about the then-predicted Y2K event at the turn of the century. When asked what he and the people in his congregation were doing to prepare for the possible crisis, he threw back his head and roared. "Oh, black folks don't have to prepare for Y2K," said Pastor Hill. "We've *lived* Y2K! We had no electricity and not much to eat. Mama had to take in wash to keep us going. She'd pray, 'Give us our daily bread,' and we'd see our 'daily bread' come in. I remember a man riding up on a horse one day after Mama had prayed, and deliverin' sacks of food—hams, turkey—enough to do us a good while. Can't tell somebody like me 'bout storin'. I've lived in the blessing of the Lord."

When your mentors speak into your life and prime the pump, God's natural law of abundance can operate. Under His watchful eye, your gifts will be blessed and multiplied until there is enough for everyone.

Watchmen on the Wall

In Bible times watchmen were positioned on top of the walls behind the gates to guard cities, or in tall watchtowers to protect vineyards, fields, and flocks. It was their job to be on the lookout for any sign of trouble on the horizon.

The requirements for watchmen include being available, alert, and armed.

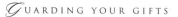

Available

The watchmen of Israel could not afford to be out chasing cows or busy in the marketplace or attending a wedding feast when they were needed for guard duty. No, everything else took second place when duty called.

A spiritual mentor who understands her calling will always be available. She will set up ways in which you can communicate quickly and freely. For this season of "guard duty" over your life, she will allow no distractions or hindrances. She will be willing to drop everything to come to your aid and to help you protect and develop the gifts God has placed in you.

Alert

With the security of a whole region at risk, watchmen could not fall asleep on the job. Nor could they chat with their comrades for fear of losing concentration. Their senses were honed razor sharp. Like members of the Secret Service, watchmen would sweep the territory with their gaze, able to detect the slightest motion in the distance. Ears were keenly tuned to their surroundings for the sound of an advancing enemy army or marauding thieves.

Spiritual mentors, like watchmen on the wall, are posted to keep a sharp eye for anything that can penetrate your defenses. They will listen and look for weaknesses from within and attacks from without. A mentor doesn't do you any favors by keeping quiet when she spots signs of impending problems. She is charged to sound the alarm.

> Sound the alarm in Jerusalem! Let the blast of the warning trumpet be heard upon my holy mountain.

Then the Lord will pity his people.... He will reply, "See, I am sending you much corn and wine and oil, to fully satisfy your need...."

Fear not, my people; be glad now and rejoice, for he has done amazing things for you.

Joel 2:1,18,21

Armed

While the role of watchmen was primarily to signal for help when an attack was imminent, some were likely equipped with weapons in case they were besieged before reinforcements could arrive.

God has not left us helpless, either. A good mentor, like Eliza, will encourage you to be prepared for skirmishes with the enemy of our souls by arming yourself with the strong Word of God. Ephesians 6:10-20 is the most comprehensive guide given for putting on battle armor. You ought to "put on the armor" each morning, along with your makeup, before you set one foot out the door.

The Belt of Truth (v. 14)

Honor and honesty go hand in hand. There is no such thing as "little white lies." A lie is a lie, and you know who is the father of liars! (John 8:44.)

The Breastplate of Righteousness (v. 14)

If we are seeking to do God's will, we will stay out of trouble. A godly lifestyle is the surest protection against evil.

The Shoes of Peace (v. 15)

Jesus is the Prince of Peace. As we go about our daily walk, we go as His ambassadors of peace in a war-torn world. Being rooted and grounded in the Lord will stabilize our steps and keep us "upright."

The Shield of Faith (v. 16)

We can't get far if we are on slippery ground. Faith calls things that are not as though they were (Rom. 4:17) and puts out all the fiery darts of the enemy.

The Helmet of Salvation (v. 17)

I'd rather be saved than sorry! If you have any doubt about your final destination, stop right here and repeat this prayer after me:

Dear Jesus, have mercy on my lost soul and forgive my sins. Take away this heavy load, this awful burden, from my heart and set me free.

Deliver me from every wrong desire and every bad habit that binds my life and, dear Lord, give me Your peace for my soul and Your power to make me God's child right now.

Dear Lord, I believe You are the Son of God and You gave Your life and rose from the dead to give me eternal life. I receive You into my heart this very moment as my Lord and Savior. I will serve You from this hour, all the days of my life. This I will do by the help of God and in the name of Jesus Christ. Amen.

The Sword of the Spirit (v. 17)

The most necessary piece of equipment in the believer's arsenal, God's Word, will renew your mind (Rom. 12:1-2) (cleanse it from accumulated garbage acquired through years of exposure to the media), will light your path (Ps. 119:105), and will give you ammunition to go on the offensive when the enemy comes to rob, kill, and destroy. (John 10:10.) Jesus' only weapon during His temptation was Scripture. He quoted His Father, and the devil retreated! (Matt. 4:1-10.) Fill your mind with God's Word, and you will be victorious in battle.

God Will Not Fail

Even your mentors, however, can fail to be always available, alert, and armed. But God, the "watcher of mankind" (Job 7:20) never fails.

> He won't let you stumble,
> your Guardian God won't fall asleep.
> Not on your life! Israel's Guardian
> will never doze or sleep.
> Yahweh's your Guardian,
> right at your side to protect you—
> shielding you from sunstroke,
> sheltering you from moon stroke.
> Yahweh guards you from every evil,
> he guards your very life.
> He guards you when you leave and when you return,
> he guards you now, he guards you always.
>
> Psalm 121 MESSAGE

The Most Popular People I Know

The most popular people I know are not sports heroes, media darlings, or the rich and famous. They are not people who demand the spotlight. They are people who have learned one of God's most valuable secrets—*the fine art of giving.*

Because I call myself a collector of friends, it should come as no surprise to you that people are my "hobby." My two most enjoyable pastimes are (1) sitting for hours in the company of a good storyteller and (2) watching successful people doing what they do best. By observing and listening, I learn.

The common thread that binds these two groups together is the fact that they are givers. We gravitate toward such people because they are willing to invest time in us. They are accessible to provide support and nurture when we need it, to network with others, to problem-solve. They give love and encouragement; they offer praise when it is merited and admonition when it is deserved. They make a place for you in their lives. Sometimes they even give some tangible expression of their affection.

Knowing of my love for flowers and having admired the ones in her garden, my friend and mentor Charlotte once sent to my mountain home a lovely clump of lilac asters, roots still intact and wrapped in moist paper toweling for replanting! I can't tell you how that gesture touched me. I have received many bouquets of cut flowers in my life, even petals from John's prize roses, which he had romantically strewn on the bed, but never has a friend sent such a unique expression of love. The bonus was that in the mountains, where it rains all the time and the conditions are just right, those asters bloomed more brilliantly and profusely than they had ever bloomed in Charlotte's garden!

That is the picture of a mentor-mentoree relationship. That which is imparted by the Lord and the mentor often thrives in the fertile soil of your unique giftings and produces a fuller and more abundant harvest. What a paradox! What a miracle!

Givers or Keepers?

There is a blessing in both giving and receiving, but there comes a time when the receiver must be more like a sieve than a sponge. God has given you specific gifts. Your mentors have imparted to you. After soaking up all these blessings, you are positioned to move in your own purpose and destiny and spread the joy.

Some women, though, are hoarders. They hang on to everything they accumulate. I know some people like that. Some of them came out of the Depression era and are afraid to let go of anything in case the economy bottoms out again. They are packrats, buying and collecting and storing up, but rarely sharing.

There are spiritual packrats as well. These people hold on to unwholesome relationships or memories they really need to release. They live in the past, rehashing old memories and pulling the scabs off old wounds. They are the victims, the spiritual recluses, preferring to stop time and close the doors to any refreshing breeze that might blow through. Like the Dead Sea, which has no outlet, they become more and more bitter—and finally they dry up.

- Givers receive. Keepers lose.

- Givers have invitations piled high; keepers have to invite themselves to the party.

- Givers receive hugs and kisses and lots of cards and letters; keepers distance themselves from others and get no mail.

- Givers are always full; keepers are never satisfied.

- A true giver does not give to receive, but that's the surprising twist: It happens anyway!

When John and I were first married, my girls were ten and thirteen. Just before Christmas, I asked if we could celebrate at Willbrook, an annual tradition we wanted to continue. Of course, he agreed.

When we arrived and walked up the eight steps onto the porch, we were amazed to see a large assortment of hams, turkeys, crates of fruit, baked goods, and every kind of edible, all beautifully bowed and wrapped for the season.

"What was all that on the porch?" John asked as we were taking off our coats inside.

"Oh, just a few Christmas gifts from some friends," I said, but I knew it was a great deal more than that. The abundance I had seen was the result of my parents' being givers. All those people who had brought food were people my parents had mentored. Mother and Daddy had done so much for others that every holiday there was a huge return on their investment.

The amusing thing is that Daddy always turned around and gave everything away. As soon as it arrived on the front porch, he was instructing the farm helpers to carry it to the back porch, where he supervised its distribution to people in need: single mothers, widows, people going through difficult times. The more he received, the more he gave—not to the people who could repay, but to the truly needy.

That is God's plan. The more you receive, the more you have to give. He is the provider, and the provision is built in. The only thing you can do to stop the provision is to step out of His will with some selfish agenda and block the blessing.

He created you to receive through revelation, His Word, the Holy Spirit, parents, teachers, and mentors. He also expects you to keep the channel open for more gifts—by giving them away.

The Greatest Gift

God is doing great and marvelous things in our midst. I personally don't want to miss a thing He has for us! Just think about it. You and I are privileged women. We are living in the greatest era of world history. We have the Word of God in our hearts, the Spirit of God to enable and equip us, and we are on the brink of seeing prophecy fulfilled in our personal lives as well as globally. It's time to give back some of what has been given.

Another story about Daddy that never fails to impact me with a greater truth is the time he was raising chickens. Even though Willbrook was primarily a cotton plantation, he was particularly fond of chickens. He would add chickens and chicken houses until there was barely room to step.

More than anything else, though, he enjoyed giving away the eggs. Two groups of people got first pick: ministers and highway patrolmen. These were men my father esteemed highly and felt deserved the best he had to offer. These families were given "picking privileges" for any of the produce grown on the farm, along with the eggs.

I can see Clara in the kitchen now—carefully washing the eggs still warm from the roosts, sorting them, then wrapping them carefully to store in brown paper sacks until they were picked up. Eggs everywhere!

Soon there were so many that Mother concocted a brilliant idea. Without saying anything to Daddy, she arranged to take them into town and sell them at the grocery store. Asking one of the workers to load her car, she decided that right after lunch, she'd take the eggs in to town and get them out of the way.

When Daddy came home for lunch, he noticed the sacks in the back seat of Mother's car and asked her about them. "Oh, it's nothing, Marshall," she said, giving an airy little wave of her hand. "Just a few eggs I'm taking in to town to leave with the grocer."

There was not a hint of condemnation in his voice, not one little sign of scolding when he said, "How much are you getting for them?"

She named the figure the grocer had offered. Without a word, Daddy reached into his back pocket, pulled out his wallet, and peeled off a few bills. At Daddy's funeral, someone said, "Marshall Williams was the only man I've ever known in the chicken business who bought his own eggs!"

I know Someone else who gave a great gift, then bought it back. When Jesus was born on the earth, He came to mentor. He chose twelve men of varying backgrounds and personalities to be His closest friends and mentorees. There were fishermen, a tax collector, a quiet man, a blustery and profane man, a zealot, a traitor. Each of them watched as the Son of God Himself modeled for him a life of holiness.

Then, almost before His ministry began, it was finished. He was crucified as a common thief. He died to fulfill God's plan of salvation, rose again, and ascended to the Father. God sent Him, used Him to show us the path to heaven, then took Him home and sent His Spirit to be our Comforter and guide. We have been bought with a great price, so we do not belong to ourselves.

Nor do our gifts belong to us. They are ours for a season—to discover, to develop, and to give away. It is when we come to this realization that we graduate from mentoree to mentor, and we are ready for commencement—the beginning of the richest and most fulfilling part of life!

Part 3

THE OPEN GATE: SPIRITUAL DAUGHTERS

And it shall come to pass in the last days,

says God, that I will pour out of My Spirit

on all flesh; your sons and your daughters

shall prophesy, your young men shall see

visions, your old men shall dream dreams.

And on My menservants and on

My maidservants I will pour out My Spirit

in those days; and they shall prophesy.

ACTS 2:17,18 NKJV

Ruth and Naomi

Some relationships are so pure and holy that it is easy for one to follow another without fully knowing where the pathway will lead! This was true of one biblical relationship between mother- and daughter-in-law, whose beautiful story is a timeless classic.

When Ruth's husband died, her trust in her mother-in-law, a woman of another faith and homeland, was so secure that she could say without hesitation, "Entreat me not to leave you, or to turn back from following after you; for wherever you go, I will go; and wherever you lodge, I will lodge; your people shall be my people, and your God, my God" (Ruth 1:16 NKJV).

With the destinies of the two women intertwined, Ruth's obedience to her mother-in-law led her to her future husband and positioned her to be a forebear of our Lord Himself!

Don't miss your next mentor. Don't fail to be obedient when she speaks. God has great and mighty things for you, works too wonderful for words.

CHAPTER 11

The Anointing

*"The Spirit of the Lord God is upon Me, because
the Lord has anointed me to preach good tidings
to the poor; He has sent Me to heal the brokenhearted,
to proclaim liberty to the captives, and the opening
of the prison to those who are bound."*

ISAIAH 61:1 NKJV

As with any graduate when school is finally out and she is facing the unknown, I left the safe cocoon of my season with Eliza and Charlotte with both anticipation and many questions. What did God have for me now? What new adventure lay ahead? What steps should I take to find my first mentoree—or should I wait on the Lord? My cup was full, and I was bursting to share it!

I am learning, however, that our creative God is constantly full of surprises. With Him, nothing is pat or predictable. On a hot July night in 1988, a friend called to say, "I'm going to take you and John somewhere that will change your lives." I was, of course, intrigued. Apparently I would have to go to "summer school" before I was fully launched into my destiny.

Our destination, of all places, was a converted dairy barn. On our way there, there were no signs or lights, and the area was heavily wooded, with only a gravel access road. One would have to have a prophetic anointing to find it!

As we worshiped in that place with the small group led by Prophetess/Pastor Mary Crum, the Spirit of the Lord was heavy. I knew that something huge was going on inside—a major transition of some kind. Whatever it was, I could hardly wait to return the next week for the second installment.

Still reeling from the impact of that worship experience, I told John on the way home, "We'll never be the same. We're moving to the next level with God." What that level would entail was still a mystery.

Pregnant With Promise

I was immediately drawn to Mary Crum. We could almost be sisters. We have the same tastes, we look a lot alike, we entertain in the same way, and we have many of the same giftings. Yet not until the second week at the Life Center did I meet her and receive any inkling of the enormous impact this woman would have on my life.

As I sat there transfixed, hearing God's heart through her words, He showed me clearly that it was He who was speaking. The music flowed, and key Scriptures were spoken over us. God's Word became life to me.

Throughout the evening, there was an ongoing silent dialogue as the Holy Spirit lavished His grace on us. And then Mary called me to the front of the group. Never having met me before and not having a clue as to my profession, she nailed the prophetic word I had been speaking intuitively to my interior design clients. "God uses you to minister to people in their homes," she said. "You go in with a discerning eye to bring beauty and order; then you tie it all up neatly with a bow. When you open your mouth, you call forth life into dead places."

I was stunned. Mary had put a name to something I had been doing for some time. In the homes of my clients, after my decorating work was done, I would say, "Now that we've pulled this house together, you'll begin to see how peace and order will come," or, "There is balance and harmony here now, and it's time to rest." It was a kind of benediction on each home.

As Mary shed light on the truth, that light started bouncing. The hair on my head literally stood up. I sat in a pool of glory, drenched in God's love as I sensed a prophetic ministry being birthed in me that night.

From Mary, I learned that *a true mentor has a humble heart but the holy boldness of the Lord.* She is anointed to activate the anointing in others. She is not arrogant about this rather dramatic aspect of ministry, but is only aware that it is a part of her God-given role. "Why is it he gives us these special abilities to do certain things best? It is that God's people will be equipped to do better work for him, building up the church, the body of Christ, to a position of strength and maturity" (Eph. 4:12). When an impartation or anointing is bestowed, the mentor does not take the credit, but gives all the glory to God. "But God forbid that I should glory, save in the cross of our Lord Jesus Christ" (Gal. 6:14 KJV).

It's a God Thing

No one can really teach you to preach or to encourage or to practice any of the gifts of the Spirit except the Spirit Himself. No one can really teach you to prophesy. Prophecy, too, is a gift of the Holy

Spirit. But you can learn how to hear from God. When an anointed prophetic activator and igniter challenges you to extend your faith to hear from God, something happens that is hard to explain to the natural mind. You begin to receive words through pictures as impressions from the Lord. You just have to acknowledge that it's "a God thing." Then His Spirit will guide you into your own unique gifting.

To "speak for God" is one of the highest callings, but it is also one of the most delicate and dangerous. (1 Cor. 14:29-40.) You must proceed along the path of prophecy with great caution. You'd better not try to speak in your own flesh, or you will be in danger! (Jer. 23:32-40.) Holy accountability is demanded of the prophet. John and I set forth on this journey with reverence for the giver and the gift.

As God quickens your understanding of the anointing for your gifts, the experience will seem almost mystical. It is the Holy Spirit who anoints, although a mentor may be the human vehicle to carry the blessing—invisible, yet more real than anything you can see with your eyes or touch with your hands.

In the Old Testament, anointing was a procedure in which people were smeared or rubbed with oil for the purpose of healing, setting apart, or embalming. That is why the physical act of anointing often involves the use of some form of oil.

From ancient times kings were ceremonially anointed as a sign of official appointment to office, and as a symbol of God's power upon them. Each king of Israel was viewed as an anointed one, someone who would deliver them from their enemies and establish the nation as God's presence on the earth.

The key words here are *God's presence* and *God's power.* Without these, nothing we do as His people can be effective or fruitful.

God's recipe for the anointing oil used in consecrating the taber-
nacle is found in an obscure passage in Exodus (30:17-33). Juanita
Bynum, writing in *Spirit-Led Woman,* interprets these elements for
twenty-first century kingdom women in ministry:

- *Myrrh:* a substance used as a purifier and as an embalming
  fluid. Christians must first be purified from their sins, then as
  dead to those sins as a corpse, unable to respond to sinful
  impulses. (Rom. 6:11-13.)

- *Cinnamon:* a sweet-smelling spice that exudes the fragrance
  of Jesus. "Be full of love for others, following the example of
  Christ who loved you and gave himself to God as a sacrifice
  to take away your sins...for Christ's love for you was like
  sweet perfume to him" (Eph. 5:2).

- *Cane (calamus):* another sweetener used in the anointing oil.
  We must be doubly sweet, overflowing with kindness, gentleness, and love, thus defusing difficult situations and dis-
  arming difficult people.

- *Cassia:* an herb planted near the banks of a river or water
  supply for survival. Our roots must go deep in the Word in
  order to be sustained in the dry season. (Jer. 17:7,8.)

- *Olive oil:* This oil is extracted under intense pressure as the
  olives are squeezed in a press. Those who seek the anointing
  must "expect to be shaken and crushed for the cause of
  Christ.... But if we persevere with an attitude of love, humility and thankfulness, the oil of the Holy Spirit will flow out
  of us to others."[1]

*These spices and oils are tangible substances representing spiri-
tual qualities.* Mentors not only model these ingredients, but also
encourage you to stir them up within yourself. Still, it is that
awesome, indescribable spiritual essence that is the true anointing.

It is a hovering of the Spirit, a brooding over your innermost being to bring forth life. Just as in the act of love out of which a child is conceived, there are very few words in our language that do justice to the experience. It's a God thing!

"Everybody Needs a Sponsor"

As an apostolic prophetess, Pastor Mary Crum, founder, along with her husband Apostle/Pastor Paul (Buddy) Crum, cofounder, established Life Center Ministries, which is a church and training-resource center to equip and empower the saints for the work of the ministry. (Eph. 4:12.)

When John and I signed up for the School for Prophetic Teams at the Life Center church, I got to know Mary better. I learned how she had come to embrace her own anointing for ministry. Her first mentor was her father, a barber, then a real estate developer in Savannah, who rejoiced with her mother over the birth of their first child after seventeen years of marriage.

From the beginning he treated little Mary like a lady, respected and honored her, and challenged her thinking. When one of his customers started him up in the building business, he never forgot the favor. From that experience came a life lesson for Mary: "Everybody needs a sponsor," her father would say, "somebody to help them get from where they are to the place they need to be." The idea of sponsoring took root at that point and nourished the rest of her life.

Her father had more for her to learn. He cultivated his daughter as a farmer nurtures his crops, as a gardener fosters the tender buds. "What's on your mind today, Mary?" he'd ask during their early-morning chats at the breakfast table. If she related some dreadful mistake she'd made the day before, he'd simply laugh and reply, "Well, what would you do if you could do it over?" At her response, he would then smile in approval. "How smart you are! You know more today than you did yesterday."

"My father taught me to take the limits off and learn from my mistakes," Mary says with gratitude. "Because of his sponsorship, I can now mentor others. It's part of the context of my life."

The best—godly men and women, all of them—have mentored Mary. One of them, Miss Rook, once said after a barrage of questions from Mary, "God's Word is anointed. Questions aren't." As Eliza did for me, Miss Rook made Mary look up the answers to her questions in the Word. "Don't look at me; look it up!" This same lady, with her customary trace of consecrated directness also said, when Mary began teaching Sunday school, "Unfortunately, you are extremely analytical. Fortunately, God can use it."

This kind of mentoring prepared Mary for the difficult road she would follow in ministry—past every kind of obstacle, harassment, and ploy of the enemy to undermine her ministry, and finally to the unlikely piece of property her husband had purchased from the former owner, the editor of Margaret Mitchell's classic novel, *Gone With the Wind*.

The barn she and her husband, Buddy, purchased, including several acres of farmland, had become extremely overgrown and hidden from view, to say the least. In fact, this property, which had been a dairy farm in the Civil War days, had been used for a very private residence for fifty years. Rustic as it was, it did have a great deal of charm and character, although it was hard to tell which walls were add-ons and which were load-bearing. There had been many additions. It would require major renovation.

While praying one day with a friend—to get some idea of what needed to be done and for understanding of the kind of training center the friend was seeing—Mary had a vision, a real visitation of the Lord. It was so real that she could smell the flowers, hear the birds singing, and feel the sun on her skin. It seemed that Jesus came and knocked on her back door, something that in the South only dear and familiar friends do.

He took her by the hand and walked her to the far end of the property. Instantly back in the barn, Jesus stood by a fireplace in front of a roomful of people who were prostrate in prayer on the floor. One by one, He pointed them out, called them up to the front, and motioned to Mary to activate their gifting.

As the vision continued, He spread His hands and said to her, "You will see what you need to see when you need to see it. You will hear what you need to hear when you need to hear it." Immediately she could see the lay of the land, covered as it was with vines and tangled underbrush. Here was a counseling house; there, a business center. A covered porch with tables was a beehive of activity, with some seated and others serving. It would be a couple of years before Mary would actually behold the fulfillment of this prophetic vision—The Life Training and Resource Center. It went from a handful of eager worshipers to hundreds of members who would be sent out in prophetic and apostolic teams to take the anointing to the nations!

Yet precious Mary will say only, "I'm just another Mary in a barn."

Reproducer of Reproducers

A breakthrough for Mary came when she was introduced to Dr. Bill Hamon, who activated and released her strong prophetic gifting and quickly became her mentor and spiritual father. A world-famous prophet and apostle, Bishop Hamon is founder and bishop of

Christians International Ministries, a network of over 300 prophetic churches. It was he who, flying in the face of popular sentiment against women pastors, used Mary to preach and to give testimony, and called her forth to speak prophetically in his conferences.

"You can't steal what's yours, what you've been given," he told her. When she confessed concern that people might think she was exhibiting too much authority over men in her role as pastor, he said, "You're not stealing the authority of the men you're leading, Mary. God called you and commissioned you to pioneer a prophetic-apostolic church in Atlanta. You were given authority. You can't steal what's yours—only walk in it."

Bishop Hamon's vision rang Mary's destiny bell. She was excited to see what God was doing through this great man and wanted to serve him. It was a modern-day replay of Paul and Timothy—except that Mary was the bishop's *daughter* in the faith. "I long to visit you," Paul wrote to Timothy, "so that I can impart to you the faith that will help your church grow strong in the Lord. Then, too, I need your help, for I want not only to share my faith with you but also to be encouraged by yours: Each of us will be a blessing to the other" (Rom. 1:11,12). Whenever Mary and Bishop Hamon minister together in seminars and other venues, they are a strong team—a double blessing.

When God decided to create mankind, there was only a pile of dirt. He blew into that dust and created Adam, then prophesied his purpose: "Be fruitful and multiply" (Gen. 1:28 NKJV). *Part of mentoring is multiplying yourself, which goes back to the Designer's original plan.* Mentoring—and I say this with utmost reverence, knowing that God is the only Creator, and we are His obedient children walking in Abba Father's footsteps—is breathing life into dry and dusty places.

Mary tells us how the impartation works. "When you impart a thing, you, the mentor in this case, take something that is a part of you and put it into someone else, the mentoree. Then the thing that is imparted becomes a part of the one to whom it was imparted."

Impartation communicates, teaches, and trains—but impartation is much more than any of those things.

Impart also means *bestow.* Now, the word *bestow* has three interesting parts. Part one is to give or present a gift. Part two is to put or place in storage, or house. Part three is to apply or use. When something is imparted, the "imparter" first gives it; it is then received and is now resident in both the "imparter" and the "impartee," and it is ready to be used or released. *The more you use the gift, the more you will have.* Just as John's roses bloom most prolifically when they are cut often, so our gifts multiply in the proportion to which they are used.

Mary tells of six ways to impart.

Ministration

There is such power in the human touch. Babies are quieted; the sick are comforted; the elderly are blessed. But think how much *more* blessing goes forth when we lay hold of God's Spirit through the laying on of hands. As God's Spirit moves in the anointing, the sick are healed (see Mark 10:18; Acts 28:8), the possessed are delivered, and the captives are set free. (See Isa. 61:1.) Laying on of hands is a means of releasing God's anointing. In Hebrews 6:2, it is set forth as a doctrine. The entire book of Acts teaches that the early church put this doctrine into practice.

Vocalization

God literally spoke the world into existence. "Then God said, 'Let there be light.' And light appeared" (Gen. 1:3). "And God said, 'Let the vapors separate to form the sky above and the oceans below'"

(v. 6). "Then God said, 'Let the water beneath the sky be gathered into oceans so that the dry land will emerge.' And so it was" (v. 9). There is power in the tongue—teaching, preaching, prophesying—but without love and the power of the Spirit it is all "sounding brass or a clanging cymbal" (1 Cor. 13:1 NKJV).

Literally, the first thing God did after He created man was to prophesy Adam's purpose to him. Impartation by vocalization can impart life to God's purpose in a person or in a people.

Association

There is also power in the company you keep—whether good companions or evil. Jesus called twelve disciples. Believers are to function as a body. "God sets the solitary in families" (Ps. 68:6 NKJV). We are not called to isolation but to community. Look at Moses and Joshua, Elijah and Elisha, Naomi and Ruth—biblical pairs who caught the mentoring vision.

Authorization

For reasons known only to our great God, He has chosen to release authority to His children. (Luke 9:1.) As Bishop Haman says, "Extend your faith and see what God is saying. Then move out in the authority He has given you."

God gave Moses authority to lay hands on Joshua and impart wisdom to him. It is true that Joshua was imparted to by association, vocalization, and every other way, but this was one time when God authorized Moses to impart wisdom to Joshua. Sometimes God will authorize a person to impart a special anointing for a certain thing.

Manipulation and control are characteristic of the Jezebel spirit. But there is a difference in hearing the Word of God and acting in His authority. Failing to do so can result in missing a blessing.

Visualization

Under the anointing, it is possible to call forth things that are not as though they were. (Rom. 4:17.) This is not witchcraft, but seeing things in the Spirit as He reveals what is hidden. A mentor might impart to a mentoree by the mentoree's watching, looking, seeing things that others might not see. The mentoree may have received an impartation to see and do or be, but may not be able to tell you how he can see or do those things.

Demonstration

What you *see being done* is key. We learn a great deal from observing how things are done—from arranging flowers to designing interiors. As a mentor imparts wisdom about how a thing is done under the anointing, the human spirit is quickened by the Holy Spirit to absorb and to grow.

Impartation by demonstration involves seeing, but it goes far beyond that. It implies involvement in the showing—observing not only *what* but *how* the mentor does something or handles situations, responds to people, or participates in life.

Breaking the Yoke

When mentorees "graduate" and achieve the status of mentors, there is a special responsibility to continue the cycle of reproduction. Stumbling into sin halts the whole process. Mentors need to keep short accounts with God: to confess quickly and to take captive every wayward thought.

For though we walk in the flesh, we do not war according to the flesh. For the weapons of our warfare are not carnal but mighty in God for pulling down strongholds, casting down argument and every high thing that exalts itself against the knowledge of God, bringing every thought into captivity to the obedience of Christ.

2 Corinthians 10:3-5

They especially need to protect their gatekeeping authority.

The gatekeepers of Israel were key to the well-being of the entire city and surrounding region. Whatever got through those gates spelled either life or death to the inhabitants.

Gates are ports of entry for demonic forces. In Atlanta many historic sites—Civil War monuments, Indian burial grounds, denominational headquarters—bear testimony to the fact that some city fathers in the past left a gate open, and unclean spirits (the spirit of witchcraft and paganism, religious spirits, the spirit of death) walked right in. Therefore, it is crucial that gatekeepers keep the faith and stay vigilant to guard their posts well.

Now is the time when God is rallying His people to break strongholds and to repent of generational sins. We need prophetic intercessors to stand in the gap and sound the alarm. John and I are excited about the assignment God has given us to use every opportunity and every platform to bring light and truth not only to our city but also to the world as we travel.

God has placed anointings within us that we don't even know. We limit ourselves by limiting His power within us. More power will come as we obey and act on the light He has given.

Under the Cloud

When the children of Israel were led out of 400 years of bondage in Egypt and began their painfully slow journey to the Promised Land, they first had to pass through the wilderness. With no compass to guide them and only a reluctant leader named Moses, they looked to God to provide tangible evidence of His presence. "Marvelous things he did in the sight of their fathers.... In the daytime also He led them with the cloud, and all the night with a light of fire" (Ps. 78:12,14 NKJV). As long as they remained "under the cloud," they were under His care and provision. When they moved out ahead or ventured off on their own side trips, disaster befell them.

To some extent, mentoring is like that. When God sends a mentor to you or launches you into a mentoring relationship with someone else, a two-way exchange takes place. While one is imparting, the other must be obedient to receive and act on the impartation. If she decides to disregard the clear word of God through His messenger, she's on her own! On the other hand, the faithful mentoree intercedes for her mentor, honors her position, and stands by to serve her.

Mary and I have moved into a mutual mentorship at this point in our lives. I am often led to pray for her when I don't have a clue as to what is going on in her life. Once I had such a burden for her that I called her husband and said, "While I was in prayer, Mary's face was before me. I don't know where she is or what's happening, but I want her to know that I'm praying. Tell her I'm going to war for her!" Only then did I learn that while ministering in Trinidad, she had become quite ill. As she says, it seems I have always been there at the critical times in her life. That is not I; that is a God thing!

Such a relationship is far more than friendship. It is a God-anointed, God-appointed relationship to accomplish His purposes in

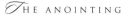

the world. It is a partnership with Him. In review, good mentors impart truth, stir up giftings, and provide a safe place for growth. Good mentorees honor and support their mentors. As long as the cloud of His presence hovers over the two of you, it is time to abide with Him in that favored place. When it lifts, the season is over, but the friendship and mutual encouragement remain.

Mary and I are in close touch, and each of us still supports and champions the other. As with Eliza, a few minutes with Mary is the essence of some rare and exotic perfume and lasts for months. Every Valentine's Day is a special day to express our love and devotion and the gratitude in our hearts for the gift of each other.

God did not leave when the cloud lifted over His people in the wilderness. He was merely signaling an end to a period of time and urging them to move on with Him to the next place. *Cherish your mentors, be on the alert for the next mentoree, but be ready to move on when the season ends.* The best part of His plan is yet ahead!

CHAPTER 12

A Daughter Speaks

Then Naomi her mother-in-law said to [Ruth],
"My daughter, shall I not seek security for you,
that it may be well with you?"
And [Ruth] said to her, "All that you say to me I will do."

RUTH 3:1,5 NKJV

I can always tell when my mother is in the house. Her fragrance floats on the very air—an essence of lotions and powders and the finest French perfumes, mingling with her own delicate scent. I can remember thinking, as a child, that my mother was the most beautiful, sweetest-smelling woman in the world. Looking at her through the eyes of innocence, I was seeing my first role model. Even her fragrance was feminine and nurturing.

Your mother's aroma may not be the essence of Joy perfume. She may smell of apple pie or flowers or even the sweat of honest toil, but her aroma is distinctive. Something about that smell will always connect you with home and your roots.

A spiritual daughter will also recognize the fragrance of her spiritual mother. Each mentor will have her own unique aroma. It will be a blending of the ingredients of her walk with the Lord—the essence of love, joy, peace, patience, kindness, goodness, faithfulness, gentleness, self-control (Gal. 5:22,23)—the fruity aroma of the Spirit in her, mingling with every pain and problem of her life to the moment you meet her.

In each case, the formula is distinctive, designed for that woman alone as an anointing for the work the Lord has for her to do. You will be able to close your eyes and breathe it in, knowing instinctively which mentor she is.

I once commented on Mary Crum's lovely fragrance and was told, "It's Knowing, by Estee Lauder!" Yes, it's *knowing*, all right, but not by Estee Lauder. God has given Mary the greatest *knowing* of all, and I can detect her presence each time I catch a whiff of it!

Even if your relationship with your natural mother is not perfect or if you have come from a broken family background, God is putting in place a spiritual mother—or maybe more than one—who will be able to lead you to redemption and healing. You will not be deprived forever. Just sniff the air. She will be wearing the most heavenly aroma. "Now thanks be to God who always leads us in triumph in Christ, and through us diffuses the fragrance of His knowledge in every place. For we are to God the fragrance of Christ" (2 Cor. 2:14,15 NKJV).

Hold My Hand

Just as your natural mother once cautioned you when crossing a busy intersection or when she perceived any kind of potential threat, your spiritual mother will say, "Hold my hand." During this phase of absorbing the deeper life with God, you are too inexperienced to move out on your own. *Your mentor has been sent to protect and to lead while you are learning the ropes.* It will save a lot of time and trouble if you simply follow.

While your own mother may be a godly example and able to nurture you in many ways, a spiritual mentor is meant to take you much further into realms of experience that are beyond human understanding. Once you glimpse the glories that await you, you will be eager to pursue this path, never disdaining the past but excited about the future.

The Wealthy Mother

Natural daughters grow up in the environment in which they are born, never really suspecting that others may not be living the same lifestyle. You accept your circumstances as the way things are.

In God's plan and timing, I was placed in a prominent family. Though we children were blessed with fine schools, summer camps, and every comfort, our parents saw to it that we understood that "to whom much is given, from him [or her] much will be required" (Luke 12:48 NKJV). Consequently, we learned early about giving and about gracious hospitality.

I learned early that true wealth is not measured in acres or dollars, but in kingdom treasures imparted by godly family members and spiritual mentors. That old saying "you can't take it with you" is totally false. You *do* take it with you! Whether you choose to go into eternity chained to sins and lifetime addictions or liberated to eternal life with Jesus is up to you. You can be a believer and squeak through the gates of heaven but have a paltry inheritance from the King of kings. Or *you can make rich deposits in your heavenly account by the life of godliness you live on earth.*

"Don't store up treasures here on earth where they can erode away or may be stolen. Store them in heaven where they will never lose their value, and are safe from thieves. If your profits are in heaven your heart will be there too."

Matthew 6:19-21

You *will* receive an inheritance. Remember, you reap what you sow. (Gal. 6:7.) Why would you want to "reap the whirlwind" when you can inherit the rich storehouses of heaven? If you don't inherit from your natural mother, you *will* inherit from your spiritual mother, Mrs. Far-Above-Rubies. Everything I have, spiritually speaking, I am imparting to my spiritual daughters. I am withholding nothing. They will get it all. Meet Pam, who will receive a rich inheritance from me.

Love Letters

Here I was, in my pink suit and pearls, author of a book titled *Social Graces,* standing before an audience on the last day of a national conference for women. There she was, a self-described "Missouri hick, formerly strung out on heroin, a woman who had lived under a bridge." We were not the most likely pairing of mentor and mentoree, but God's idea of a great duo.

Pam is my newest daughter of the heart. God connected us that spring weekend, and we have been carrying on an e-mail correspondence ever since. When I think of what she has gone through, it is not just my mother's heart that rises up in outrage, but a holy passion that God has planted in me to protect, defend, and aid the flow of healing to her wounded spirit. Because we believe that her testimony will bring glory to God, she has graciously given us permission to share a part of her amazing story with you.

Sent: Wednesday, March 07, 2001
Subject: Women's Conference
Dear Sister Ann,

God bless you! My name is Pam, and I attended the conference last week. I was greatly touched by your message Saturday morning. Three years ago Jesus saved me and delivered me from heroin addiction and satanic practices, which involved animal sacrifices and spell-casting. Because of my lifestyle and the mental abuse I put my three boys through, my first husband obtained custody of the children, took away all my rights as their mother, and took them back to Missouri to live. I have seen them one time in three and a half years. Ever since my losing the boys, the devil has literally tormented me with nightmares. The guilt I was carrying was so unbearable I felt as though I would go crazy. There had been a loneliness in me that nobody seemed to understand, an anger I didn't know how to stop from rising up in me.

When you prayed for me, I felt a touch in my heart that I can still feel today. When you put your hand on my heart, I felt a shock go through my heart. I am thirty-six and have had two heart attacks, so I know what a shock feels like. The Holy Ghost has jump-started my heart! Praise God! I thought I would be hurt over my babies the rest of my life. But praise God, He has set me totally free and has told me that I will see my children and be part of their lives, the way He intended.

I'll never forget meeting you. You gave me a Holy Ghost hug that was just full of the love of God, and I just wanted to thank you for that hug. I have prayed for two years for the Lord to put me in touch with a woman who could help me learn about being a lady and social graces, so I am buying your book this week, Sister Ann. You are a blessing and a very precious person to me. I am praying for you and your ministry every day. I do not have a lot of money, but I would like to send you a little every month to help you take your message to others and touch their lives with the anointing of God.

Love in Jesus' holy and mighty name,
Pam

I recognized this woman's name. Margo and I had met her and her husband at the airport, standing in the outside baggage check-in. She had introduced herself, poured out her astonishing story, and expressed her gratitude for blessing her during the conference. Out of all those four or five thousand conferees, she had been one of only a few to say thank you. I had been carrying her in my heart ever since. We had bonded from the moment our eyes met. It was more than an encounter; it was God's kiss—a benediction on the weekend dedicated to Him.

Sent: Wednesday, March 07, 2001
Subject: Re: Women's Conference
Precious Pam,

Your dear letter touched the depths of my heart. What a joy to receive it today. As I told you in Tulsa, God is the ultimate refiner. He is burning out the past and redeeming the present. Your children will be restored to you. You will hold them to your breast as I held you.

I am sending you my books The Best Is Yet to Come *and* Social Graces. *This is a gift from my heart to yours.*

Bless you as you go in your new freedom. I close with this prayer:

May a Holy Ghost blessing come over you and your husband. I pray that God will continue to heal you and raise you up as a woman of honor and grace, in Jesus' name. Amen.

Thank you for your tender heart.
Love,
Ann

Sent: Sunday, March 11, 2001
Subject: (no subject)
My Dearest Sister Ann,

It is a beautiful day today! Praise God! I wanted to share something with you and have you pray for me and with me. On April 19, I am getting ordained. (It is my birthday, too, so it will be very special to me.) This is something the Lord wants me to do, and I take it very seriously. I dearly love the lost souls and so desire to see them saved and set free.

Love and blessings in Jesus,
Pam

Sent: Monday, April 02, 2001
Subject: Re: (no subject)
Dear Pam,

I am thrilled that you are being ordained in ministry on April 19. I will be praying for you at this very special time of impartation. God bless you, dear Pam. This is the beginning of the restoration of your life. Get ready, girl!

I am praying for your three children...for God to bless them and open the door for you to see them. Write me soon.
Ann Platz

Sent: Tuesday, May 08, 2001
Subject: Praise the Lord
Dearest Ann,

I just wanted to write you a quick note to let you know that I love you and am praying for you. God is moving so mightily here. The night I became ordained, two women I know and a coworker from my work got saved. God is so wonderful! I also want to let you know that on June 12, I am going to pick up my youngest son for six weeks and will get to see my other two sons for the rest of the summer. What a mighty God! Words could not describe the joy I am feeling. This is such a miracle of Jesus—only He could do this!

Love and blessings,
Pam

Sent: Tuesday, May 08, 2001
Subject: Re: Praise the Lord
Dear Pam,

How wonderful to hear from you today! I am thrilled that you will be spending time with your sons soon. You were part of the *"prayer for reconciliation with your children"* at the women's conference in March. This is a powerful answer to prayer for you. I praise God for His mercy and goodness.

Love,
Ann

Sent: Sunday, May 13, 2001

Subject: Re: Praise the Lord

Dear Ann,

God bless you! I received two cards on e-mail from my two oldest sons. How special it is to receive anything from them. I just can't wait until next month.

Today I found out I have a spinal disease. The doctor said I would need surgery on at least two vertebrae, and there is some kind of tumor growing there, too. We are praying for total healing. He wanted to take me off work until surgery, but I refused. Since I am the manager at the restaurant, I can't just leave.

Blessings,
Pam

Sent: Sunday, May 13, 2001

Subject: Re: Praise the Lord

Dear Pam,

I pray that God heals your spine, that the spirit of infirmity is removed from you and your family, and that your health is restored to you. I pray that you walk in divine health and that the healing presence of God manifest Himself to you. Thank You, Lord, for the restoration of Pam's children. THAT IS AWESOME!

Expect miracles, Pam. They are on the way.

God is speaking to me about you. He is bringing healing to you in the area of your self-image. Expect a big change in how you feel about yourself. People are going to be bringing makeup to you and they will not know why. God is bringing *a refiner's fire to you. You will bring many into the kingdom for such a time as this. Enjoy what is about to happen. It will signify the presence of God in your destiny.*

I release the joy of the Lord over you this day, Pam. Laugh and sing...rest and play. God is restoring the years the locust has eaten. He is bringing your children home to you and releasing a new anointing: THE MOTHER'S ANOINTING TO LOVE.

With love and affection,
Ann

Sent: Sunday, June 03, 2001
Subject: Catching up with Pam
Dear Ann (or could I say Mom),

We have been in revival for twelve days and God has saved nine souls, healed two of cancer, healed three knees, two warts, a hernia, stomach ulcers, and several cases of the flu. What an honor and blessing to be pastoring this church! Please continue to pray for me as I will not be picking up my children now. The devil is really trying to get me depressed, and I refuse to let him. Their father needs Jesus, not my getting angry at him. I am fasting and praying for him because I will not go back to unforgiveness and anger. Coming from devil worship, abuse, and drug addiction, I cannot allow this to stop the flow of the Holy Spirit.

You have become like a mother to me, Ann, and I am ready to go to war for you and with you in the spirit, for your ministry, for the book you told me about, for your family, and just for you.

(As I read these lines, I thought, *Oh my goodness! God is showing Pam my heart—the very core of me.* She continued,)

I am thankful to have such a lady of God to stay in touch with.

God bless you, Mom, and remember that I love you.
Pam

In that moment I realized that I had given birth to a woman who would become a mighty intercessor for me. Her heart of gratitude was touching the deepest places in my own heart. As a spiritual daughter, she knew she needed to bless me. From now on, we would be locked together for eternity.

Sent: Wednesday, June 06, 2001

Subject: Praising the Only True and Living God

Good morning, dear daughter Pam,

The Lord awakened me this morning around 3:00 and told me to go downstairs to the computer. I pulled up your e-mail and read it and cried. You have such a precious, tender heart, and I felt it all the way.

Thank God, you see the vision of the importance of spiritual mentoring. Father God sends mentors to you...you do not go out and find them or select the ones you think you need. When you recognize that it is one of the most powerful relationships that you can have as a believer...then you open yourself up to receive mightily from an anointed person of God to give you what she has for you from the Father. Add that to what you already have...and wow! People who are called to leadership by God have to have this blessing and impartation from people of wisdom...it is a legacy gifted from God the Father to His children.

Wonderful news about the revival in your church...it is God's timing for this! Miracles galore! You will feel your body begin to heal as the ministry increases in power.... It is part of the outpouring that will come.

You are a precious daughter, Pam. I love you and care for you in the way a mother loves her child. I will stand with you and mentor you for the season that God calls for me to be with you. Then He will raise up another to take you to the next level. We will always be connected, though, in Him.

Your children are fine. God is showing me that they are at peace. He is going to bring them to you. Stay sweet, and trust God with them. I release the healing anointing over you this day and pray that the tumors be dissolved and that you be set free.

May God richly bless and keep you. May His face shine upon you, Pam, and give you peace, both now and forevermore.

Your mother loves you,
Mom Ann

Sent: Tuesday, June 05, 2001
Subject: Praising the Only True and Living God
Dear Ann,

You have sent me many letters that I have just sat down and cried over. Thank you for your kindness and love of the Lord Jesus you have for me. It is worth more than any treasure on earth. Truly, no amount of money can buy the godly bond that has begun between you and me.

I know that God has connected us in His Spirit, and I am so grateful. I value all of your advice and wisdom and just love staying in touch with a Spirit-filled woman who is sold out to the Lord. I am in a season of fasting and prayer for you. I am not that grown in the lord, but I love Him and love to pray. He has given me a burden to pray for you and your ministry and family.

Lord Jesus, I ask You to bless my sister, mentor, and spiritual mom with your wisdom. Let the Holy Ghost write every page of this book and give her a double portion of strength and wisdom each and every day. So let Your will be done concerning this ministry. In Jesus' name.

P.S. My own mother never told me that I was a good daughter. Thank you for thinking that way about me. It made me weep as I realized that God loves me in that way too. Sometimes I cry for no reason at all. It is like I have been in a pressure cooker.

Maybe it is just God releasing the pressure of all the past years. I don't know... I just know the bond I feel with you I have never had even with my own father and mother...

> *Lots of love and blessings to you,*
> *Your daughter,*
> *Pam*

Sent: Tuesday, June 12, 2001

Subject: Sweet Daughter

Dear Sweet Daughter,

You are a dutiful and darling daughter, Pam. Thank you for your prayers and fasting in my behalf. I believe that you are going through a time of healing and cleansing from the Spirit of the Lord. This is the work of the Holy Spirit in the deepest parts of your mind...restoring and setting things straight that are being made whole through the Word that is alive in you. It is exciting and awesome at the same time.

Pam, I know this may sound silly, but I want you to soak in the bathtub in some bubble bath. This is your mama speaking. I want you to put moisturizing cream on your skin...nurture your body! God is preparing you for a ministry of miracles, daughter! GET READY! Prepare...you cannot give what you do not have! You will nurture many who are parched from life's pain and hurt.

I love you,
Mom Ann

Sent: Thursday, June 14, 2001

Subject: My Precious Mom

Dearest Mom,

I am taking your advice about the bubble baths. They are really relaxing, and I love them. God has been helping me because I have had a fear of bathrooms because that was where some abuse first happened to me when I was six years old. But now I can stay in my bathroom ten minutes, which is more than I ever could before.

Your letter has me in tears. God is just really tearing down walls of bitterness in me that I never knew I had. It is so easy to receive from you. It was never like this with my real mother. I really love you. You are nicer and more caring than my real mother was. I feel like you really are my mother! I am so blessed by your words of encouragement and correction. I have never had anyone I could just be myself with that accepted me for who I am, as you do.

I love you, Mama,
Pam

Pam and I may be at opposite ends of the social and educational spectrum, but we have in common the most important bond—the love of Jesus and a call to kingdom work!

The ending to our story has not been written.

Daughters of the Heart

As a little girl, when asked what I wanted to be when I grew up, I had only one answer: "A mommy." Playing with my dolls in their cradles and cribs and baby carriages, I was a good "mommy." I took care of my "children," made sure they were tucked into bed, and gave them their bottles. All of my babies were good—because they were not *real!*

Now that I have become a woman, with daughters of my own, I realize that playing with dolls is scant preparation for the reality of motherhood. I have had my struggles with my own flesh and blood. A daughter who defies all rules causes a mother to seek the Lord with all her heart. But strangely enough, the rebellion of this one daughter has enriched my prayer life, sent me to the Word, and humbled me. I have had to release her to the Lord and go to war for her many times.

Maybe that is why the Lord has called me to mentor. I am doing for other women's children what I would hope others would do for mine. So when Pam's e-mails began coming, I knew that God was using me to mentor her. It is a joy to impart wisdom and revelation to her. She "gets it"! What is unique about our relationship is the ease and speed with which she has grown. My "daughter" has now become my intercessor.

Being a mentor on the move—speaking, writing, numerous radio and TV interviews—I need the covering Pam so willingly provides. As I enter into another phase of my life, the climate around me has changed in proportion to her prayers for me.

We are both reaping huge benefits. As she shares so transparently and with vulnerability, God moves into my giftings and allows me to tell her how uniquely important she is to the tapestry of life; then she begins to get a glimpse of the glories God has for her. As she invests in my ministry, fasting and praying, she benefits again. God will reward her for her diligence. I, on the other hand, receive blessings untold—the joy of impartation, strength for my journey, and the satisfaction of seeing a daughter do well.

When your mentor shines the light of God's love and truth into your life, you will be able to walk out of the darkness of insecurities, heartache, and abuse. Your "adopted," grafted-in mother will take your hand, remove the veil and the grave clothes, and usher you into the presence of the Lord, where there is healing and wholeness. You will be totally set free. The death sentence is lifted! Hallelujah!

CHAPTER 13

Multiple Births

"I will bless her richly, and make her the mother of nations.
Many kings shall be among [her] posterity."

GENESIS 17:16

It is Eliza who likes to say, "I have many daughters I did not give birth to." And so do I. As I absorbed the impartation of many mentors and became heavy with the harvest, I longed to share the increase with other women. One by one, God led them to me—a gift from His heart to mine. Each one was heaven-sent, my spiritual daughter.

These women could have resisted the little tug to become vulnerable, to open the tightly closed buds of their hearts to blossom in the warmth of God's love—and mine. Some did resist, no doubt, and missed the blessing He had for them. Others listened well and heard the still, small voice saying, "She is yours for a season. Learn from her. You will not have her always. But I am with you. 'I will never leave you nor forsake you'" (Heb. 13:5 NKJV).

Despite Eve's deception, God has always trusted women with His most priceless treasures. He chose a woman (Mary) to cradle the Spirit seed of His only Son in her womb. He chose another woman, Mary of Magdala, from whom Jesus cast seven demons (Luke 8: 2,3), to carry the good news of His resurrection back to the other disciples. Deborah, the prophetess of Israel, sat under a tree and dispensed wisdom and justice in a time when "everyone did what was right in his own eyes" (Judg. 17:6 NKJV).

It is often easier to impart truth to spiritual daughters than to natural daughters. There is a tendency on the part of your own flesh and blood to want to dispute your word or to argue. But spiritual daughters are usually desperate seekers. They are looking for someone to tell them the truth. When God makes the connection, holy sparks fly between you, and a new bond is born that is as close as breath.

Linda is one of those special daughters.

Warrior at the Gate

When I met Linda, she was involved in a four-year affair with a prominent business official. When John and I "happened" to bump into them after church one day, I knew that God had positioned me in that pew for Linda's sake. They asked us to join them for lunch.

Afterward, as we were leaving to go our separate ways for the afternoon, I put my arms around her. "God has great plans for you," I said, giving her a knowing wink.

I'll let Linda tell you, in her own words, what happened next.

"Ann was a warrior woman at the gate, standing guard over my very bruised spirit. I had walked out of a divorce with nothing. Now, as I was ending another unhealthy relationship, Ann was there. She never criticized or faulted me. Nothing I had ever done in my rebellious past seemed to faze her. I craved that kind of acceptance and hope for my life.

"When she asked me to attend a worship service at the Life Center in Atlanta, I jumped at the chance. I would have done anything she said. The first prophetic word spoken to me was electrifying:

'Like a pebble dropped in the water, God says, you will be My Holy Ghost pebble, and I am going to drop you in the right place at the right time; and what I have for you will affect you and will affect others around you, but it will go far beyond you, far beyond a little bit. You know how the pebble ripples on out. You are going to be my Holy Ghost pebble and the ripples of that will even reach to the other shore. Amen.' How was I going to affect others?

"The answer was Ann Platz. At the Life Center I learned the purpose for which God had created me: 'To support you in receiving honesty so that clarity is realized, faith is demonstrated, confidence arises to know your purpose and value, enabling you to be free to choose life and transformation with enthusiasm for progression toward the fulfillment of your destiny.' That's also the definition of a mentor. And it didn't take long for me to realize that Ann was the one God had sent to help me reach that goal.

"She encouraged me to take a prophecy class at the Life Center. I was excited about learning more about the prophets—or so I thought. But after a brief teaching session, the instructor said, 'Everyone get a partner and let's stir up the gifts inside of us.' *Gifts? What gifts?* Then Deb said, 'Everyone pray in tongues.' I stood there, paralyzed. I couldn't speak Spanish; I couldn't pray in Latin. *Lord, I begged, I can't fake this even if I want to. If You'll get me out of this place, I will never come back!*

"When I called Ann in tears and told her what had happened, she said, with her sweet southern accent, 'Darling I didn't know you hadn't received the baptism of the Holy Spirit.' So, at her invitation, I visited the Platzes' mountain home that weekend. Everything I picked up to read, everything I heard or saw let me know that my heavenly Father was truly there. When Ann and John prayed over me, I knew something huge was happening in my spirit. My whole body trembled uncontrollably, and again the tears flowed—along with the heavenly language that my Father had stored up for me.

"As Ann began to impart my purpose and destiny in the Lord, I finally got a clue as to what I was doing here on this planet.

> O Lord, you have examined my heart and know everything about me. You know when I sit or stand. When far away, you know my every thought. You chart the path ahead of me, and tell me where to stop and rest. Every moment, you know where I am.

> You saw me before I was born and scheduled each day of my life before I began to breathe. Every day was recorded in your Book! How precious it is, Lord, to realize that you are thinking about me constantly!... And when I waken in the morning, you are still thinking of me!
>
> Psalm 139:1-3,16-18

"The veil was lifted! Rather than dreading the sunrise, now I was eager to find out what every day held."

Life on a Silver Platter

Linda continues, "I was soon to experience my first taste of the feast God was preparing for me. A woman's conference in the inner city of Atlanta was scheduled for October, and I was asked to coordinate the conference. They expected 300 people to attend! With a limited budget, we were not able to do any advertising, and I was getting a little worried about how I was going to print the brochures for the conference. God sent the answer in the form of a lady who walked up to me at church and asked if she could do anything to help. When I explained my concern, she told me that her husband was a graphic artist and that he would take down the information and get right to work. By the next day a beautiful brochure was delivered to me in the parking lot of Uptons!

"I was getting nervous about the food, too. How could we possibly feed that many? Somehow, through God's networking system, the word got out. On the day of the conference, the food began coming in, brought by women from churches and organizations all over the city. My friend Libby had arranged with a local grocery store to provide bread, angel food cake, strawberries, and bags full of salad.

"Nice start, but what about the main course? I began to relax as someone else brought a five-pound tub of chicken salad and another of egg salad. Still, we hadn't given much thought as to how we were going to serve all that food.

"That's when Ann's gifts for decorating and hospitality—and her amazing love for people of every background—swung into action. She came in, bringing her finest silver trays and huge silver punch-bowls for the salad. When the tables were set up and those beautifully arranged trays were placed, I cried. In fact, I cried all day long as I watched God cater that event!

"An intercessory prayer team of twenty women had been at work ahead of time. We had prayed once a week for six months for this conference. Under that canopy of anointing, the speaker stepped into a place of protection, and every woman played her part. The Lord was showing me one more thing—that by serving these inner-city women, using Ann's lovely heirloom silver, He was demonstrating that He wanted to give them abundant life. Life—on a silver platter!"

Blood 'n' Fire

Linda was learning that the power of mentoring is life-changing. Her second mentor would lead her into a healing and deliverance ministry. When there was no money for the classes, a scholarship was provided, and Linda received the evidence that God, like a good father, cares for His own.

As she grew spiritually, she began seeing things she had never seen before. Layers of rejection and insecurities from the past were exposed so that healing could begin. "It was like peeling an onion," she says. "I found out that my ancestors came over on the Mayflower, and I was part of the Mayflower heritage. One of my ancestors had been a deacon in the church—and the other one had been caught stealing pigs! I felt like a hog thief, too. God doesn't make mistakes. He places us in just the right families to accomplish His purposes. After all, Jesus descended from a line that includes Rahab, the harlot!" (Matt. 1:5.)

Linda's son Robert was another matter. When he got into trouble with drugs, she had begged God, "Show me how *You* see him and not how *I* see him." His answer seemed to come in the form of a question: *Do you know how many hairs there are on Robert's head? Well, I do.* (Luke 12:7.) *That's how much I love him.*

Linda was fed up with Robert's bad choices, his companions, the whole nine yards. She had done everything from praying for him to counseling him. Nothing seemed to help. One night as she was weeping before the Lord, she asked, "Lord, what do I do now?" And the still, small voice answered, *Let Me have him. Let Me have him.*

She says, "When the Lord spoke to me, I felt such a release and turned my son over to Him.

"When Robert moved out on his own, I prayed every day for God to cover him in the blood of Jesus and to keep him safe. The Lord would wake me all hours of the night. I would walk the floor, praying for my son's protection. I reminded the Lord of His promise that if

one in our household is saved, then all of the household will be saved. (Acts 16:31.) I prayed that God would bring Robert into His kingdom to become the mighty man he was called and purposed to be.

"When Robert hit rock bottom, he came to me for help. He told me about horrible nightmares in which God was allowing him to see what could happen to him if he didn't change, and it scared him."

There was only one place to turn for help at this point—a place called Blood 'n' Fire, the inner city ministry where Linda had seen God multiply the loaves and fishes! "Ron," she told the men's director, "I want my son to go through your program. He needs deliverance. I want him to know the Father as he's never known Him before. I want him to come face to face with God." She felt like Abraham, placing her son on the altar, but she was learning to relinquish and to trust God. Now she was trusting Him with the most precious person she had left.

"Before I took Robert to Blood 'n' Fire," Linda says, "I told his daddy, 'It's time to stand up and give glory to God. Remember: We are overcomers by the word of our testimony and the blood of the Lamb.' (Rev. 12:11). I left him there, not expecting to hear anything for a week or two.

"Within twenty-four hours, I had a call from Robert's counselor, Mike. 'He's not going to stay. He's ready to leave. I'll take him downstairs and you can pick him up at the loading dock.' I was panic-stricken! Was there no hope for him? Had they given up on him too? And then I realized that the inner city where they would be releasing my son was not the safest area of Atlanta. *'Oh, God, I prayed, You've got to help me! Please put Your angels around Robert until I can get there!'*

"Forty-five minutes later, I pulled up in the parking lot of the warehouse. I spotted Robert right away. He was talking with a homeless man wearing tattered clothes. At his feet was a dog. The words *angel unaware* flitted through my mind. (See Hebrews 13:2).

"As Robert transferred his things to the back seat of my car, I rolled the window down. The man reached over and gave me his hand. It was soft and his touch was gentle—not the hand of a homeless person. I thought instantly of my granddaddy who had passed away when I was sixteen.

"'You take good care of him,' he said. 'Take care of yourself too.' Then, as if reading my mind, he added, 'My name is Mr. Frank. I walk the streets of Atlanta, just reminding folks that God loves them.'"

"When the man shuffled off, his dog at his heels, I turned to Robert. His complexion was the color of ashes. 'Robert, where did Mr. Frank come from?'"

"Robert shrugged. 'I don't know, Mom. All I know is he and the dog just showed up when I got here. Mom, he started telling me my whole life story. He has more wisdom than anyone I've ever known. He even told me God's plan for my life!'

"I started to drive away, and Mr. Frank and his dog disappeared. I was trembling as I told Robert, 'Your granddaddy's name was Franklin Joel Anderson, and everywhere he went, his dog followed. He wore old clothes just like the ones Mr. Frank was wearing. Did he say what his dog's name was?' Robert couldn't remember, but a couple of nights later, he told me that the conversation was beginning to come back to him. 'Mom,' Robert said, 'Mr. Frank called his dog *Boy*. Again my spine tingled. Through tears of awe and joy, I stared at my son. 'Robert, your granddaddy's dog's name was Boy. There was a long moment when we just looked at each other before Robert said, 'Mama, God didn't just send Mr. Frank to me; He sent him to you, too.'"

Angelic visitation, or simple human kindness? Both Robert and Linda are convinced that God arranged for that divine encounter. Later, Pastor Mary explained to Linda: "You know that Mr. Frank was not your granddaddy, don't you? That was the Lord allowing Mr. Frank to represent the blessing of your grandfather."

And even that is not the end of the story. Robert was instantly delivered from drugs. God opened the door for Linda to take her son to the Life Center, where he received his first prophetic word. Through Catherine, God told Robert that the enemy had tried to take him, but that he was marked and sealed with God's own seal. We expect great things from Robert. Everything in his life will be a testimony to the faithfulness of his Father. Everything he thought he had lost is being restored. He even started working at a new job!

What if God had not positioned me to meet Linda at a critical turning point in her life? What if she had not hearkened to the voice of the Lord? A seed was sown that day that has borne more fruit than any of us could have imagined!

If we choose not to walk in God's ways, that decision will affect future generations. But if we choose life in Him, blessings will fall like rain to the third and fourth generation!

As this book is being written under the anointing of the Holy Spirit, God is revealing Himself in everyday encounters and in the supernatural. Our interview with Linda began on a Saturday. By Tuesday of the following week, her ongoing prayer for her son had been answered— just in time to make the deadline for this book! God wants you to know that He is actively participating in the lives of His children!

Handle With Care

The relationship between a mentor and a mentoree is highly sensitive and charged with spiritual energy. Much sharing, of a delicate and confidential nature, is often done. Therefore, the enemy can come into this atmosphere of emotional tension and stir up trouble, particularly if the parties are of the opposite sex. That is what happened to one of my mentorees and is why I strongly recommend that women, as a general rule, seek the counsel of other women. (See Titus 2.) There may be rare exceptions.

Jean is one of those exceptions. Left spiritually battered after a tragic experience with a male counselor and before she could reestablish trust with any other man in ministry, she needed someone who could cancel out the negative experience. For a season, the Holy Spirit led her to a committed family man, a professional with a sense of stability and purpose. Even while she was being mentored by him, Jean asked for input from other women, which provided a system of checks and balances. "In the multitude of counselors there is safety" (Prov. 11:14 NKJV).

I came along after Jean's healing was well underway to put the finishing touches on her restored "house" in the "finishing school" of the Holy Spirit. She explains it in this way: "I see Ann as a refining mentor. I need her touch, to learn from her the social graces so that I will have confidence with people from all walks of life. I feel that the Lord is preparing me for something, and Ann is in my life to impart the knowledge of how to bow before queens.

"This mentoring dynamic is so important. It's not about how to use the right fork or even how to look up the book of Obadiah in the Bible. There is an anointing in a true mentoring relationship, and I need to be very, very attentive when my mentor speaks, to listen

between the lines, to hear the heart, to see the vision of who I am in the Lord through my mentor's eyes. Though a close friend accepts you the way you are, a mentor is not satisfied. That person is in your life to take you from where you are to where you need to be. I now have a sense, through someone else's clearer vision, of progressing to the place God has intended for me in the body of Christ.

"Now I have caught that vision—and another one, too. I see a kids' playground, with connecting rods all over the place. People are strapped, spread-eagled, to the rods, all tied to the structure, yet close enough to touch and help each other. I see the Lord Himself untying one person's right wrist. That person then reaches over to untie the wrist or ankle of the nearest person, and the cycle repeats itself until everyone is free."

I see this amazing vision as revealing that no mentor is perfect! We are all in the process of becoming, of being "finished." As Jean says, "No mentor has it all together, but we can all reach out and help others with our limitations." By setting Jean free, the Lord has released a mighty woman of God to help other captives find their freedom. And the cycle of reproduction goes on.

CHAPTER 14

Becoming a Grandmother

*I know how much you trust the Lord, just as your
mother Eunice and your grandmother Lois do; and
I feel sure you are still trusting him as much as ever.*

2 TIMOTHY 1:5

I am definitely not one of those women who try to hide their ages! Actually, with my belief that "the best is yet to come," I am rather proud of each new year I acquire on the road to grace and godliness. The grandmother of three extraordinary grandchildren—Ivey, Dickson, and Morris—and John's fine grandsons, Jonathan and Jeremy, I will whip out my billfold at the drop of a hat to display the latest pictures. God truly saved the best for last when he created grandchildren.

As I have been privileged to experience the role of mentoree to some exceptional women and, later, mentor to many spiritual daughters, I have learned that the cycle of reproduction repeats itself in the spiritual realm just as it does in the natural world. Therefore, I am thrilled when I hear that one of my spiritual daughters has passed on to someone else the nuggets she gleaned from me. That makes me a spiritual grandmother many times over. Rather than feeling threatened or replaced, I rejoice that the Lord has used me as an open conduit of His love and truth. What I could never accomplish as one woman is accomplished through divine multiplication.

Frequently I will call my precious friend and mentor Mary Crum and say to her, "Would you like to hear what you and I did for the Lord today?" Learning how she has impacted someone through the truth she revealed to me never fails to bless her.

In the same way, I delight in hearing about the extension of my ministry through the daughters God has given me: a former prostitute, a businesswoman, a minister's wife, a completed Jew, the wife of a prominent CEO, an office assistant, and so many others. From every background and every rung of the social ladder they have come, and now they are reaching others within their distinctive spheres of influence. The ripples continue to widen.

Daughter of Zion

As a little girl, Suzanne wanted to be a rabbi when she grew up. She was brilliant and beautiful, a true Jewish princess. Her parents, like most good Jewish families in this country, stressed setting high achievement goals, academic excellence, and prosperity.

Indeed, Jewish people are among the best in many fields of endeavor. In his book *What the Church Owes the Jew,* Leslie Flynn writes:

> If an anti-Semite decided to boycott all the tests and cures discovered by the Jews, he would certainly open himself to a host of serious diseases. Besides refusing Jonan Salk's polio vaccine, he would also decline the polio pill by Dr. Albert Sabin; the test to fight diphtheria invented by Bela Schick...blood transfusions made possible by the work of Dr. E. J. Cohen of Harvard...the Wasserman test for syphilis...strepto-mycin discovered by Dr. Selman Abraham Waxman....

U. S. Jews are twice as likely to go to college as Gentiles, five times more likely to be admitted to an Ivy League school, and are over-represented in the fields of medicine, science, law, and dentistry.[1]

This is Suzanne's natural heritage, although she hadn't learned all she was to know about her spiritual heritage when I first knew her.

Suzanne and I met several years ago at a Bible study held in the home of a member of the country club where her fiancé, John, was a golf pro.

I'll let her tell you the rest of the story.

"While the man leading the Bible study kept scrambling for his notes, this woman sitting across the room from John and me was making profound comments. We looked at each other in awe, mentally agreeing that she should be doing the teaching. It was Ann. She had a way of getting to the crux of the matter that breathed life into what had been only a dry and dusty lecture. I was hungry for righteousness; she intrigued me from the very beginning.

"Not just anyone could have met me at the gate. God handpicked Ann for me—a woman of keen intelligence, successful in her field, with a sincere love for Jewish people. A woman who believed God's Word. Even though I had embraced Jesus as the Messiah at the age of thirteen, I was already pretty burned out on the organized church with their laundry lists of prayer requests, their programmed worship, and their 'religious' Christianity. Christian legalism was no better than what I had left: following a strict set of rules. When Ann talked about God, it was fresh manna. She gave us the big picture, magnifying the Lord in every word she spoke and everything she did.

"When there was a problem at the golf club, we called Ann. She laid hands on us and prayed—a prayer of power and authority and knowing. No ifs, ands, or buts! The problem John had had with a colleague was nailed by a prophetic word she gave that night. Needless to say, there was no conversation in the car going home. This was a major breakthrough for both of us. When the prayer was answered shortly afterward, I knew I had been in the baby pool long enough. It was time to dive into the deep end.

"As I continued to observe Ann's life, I found the kindness, gentility, and graciousness that was lacking in my own. Oh, I could be outwardly nice when the occasion called for it, but what I was seeing in her was a woman who truly honored other people, calling them by their first names—from the checkout girl at the grocery store to the sales clerk at the decorating shop. *She really does care about all those people,* I marveled. It went way beyond good manners or social graces. This was something that came from somewhere deep within...or up above...

"When John and I got married and Hurricane Hugo struck Charleston, we moved our wedding to Atlanta. Ann helped us through that crisis and the next: decorating our new home. We went from seriously tacky bachelor stuff to a more refined and sophisticated look. 'Why not paint this wall yellow, and hang some blue and white plates?' she suggested, which produced instant beauty. One thing I've learned: If you hang around beautiful things and beautiful people long enough, it will rub off on you.

"The next crisis arose before the birth of one of my children—when my mother-in-law wanted to interject herself in the involvement with the upcoming grandchild's birth. She was unintentionally stressing me with her expectations and control. Ann's wisdom brought me through. She simply prayed, 'Lord, break off this spirit of control. That mother needs to let go.' To me, she said, 'Suzanne, as a wife you are to leave and cleave, and your husband needs to do the same. We'll pray for him.'

"To my absolute amazement, without a word from me, no nagging or whining, John went to see his mother before the baby was born. When he walked in, as he told me later, he said, 'Mother, you and I have got to talk.' She knew what was coming. 'Don't make me choose between you and Suzanne. If you do, you'll lose. We have to honor her decision here. She's having the baby.' Guess what? These relationships and priorities fell into their proper places. You can't believe what that did for our marriage!

"Meanwhile, all the girls in my carpool were looking on in openmouthed awe. They could literally see the difference, and they wanted to know where I was getting all this wisdom. As our marriage began to mature and thrive—now that my husband was tending to me—all of a sudden, my friends were getting blessed. Even one living on the fumes of a previous 'religious' experience, got her second wind. If I had not been listening to Ann before, this was the credibility test. She passed with flying colors.

"What Ann does for me is what every good mentor can do: She recognizes that every decade presents a different challenge. Since she knows the landscape, having been there before me, she can show me the map of the terrain and save me a lot of grief. In fact, she has given me her own set of blueprints for the pathway to righteousness. It's not just nice Bible words and sweet prayers; it's Spirit and life! This woman is a goldmine of God's truth. All I need to access it is a teachable spirit.

"She doesn't mind being tough with me, either, so in turn, I do the same for the women in my circle of acquaintances, as the Lord leads them to me. She is always elevating my husband, and if I ever complain about something he's said or done, she gives me a gentle adjustment. We are to respect our husbands, never saying anything negative or demeaning about them, especially to our girlfriends. In fact, we are to put a hedge of protection and privacy around our husbands: no gossip, no jawboning with others about things of no value.

"Now the Lord has given me some additional words to pass on when someone is griping about a marital problem: 'You made a pledge when you got married. Remember that?' I remind them. 'Start honoring. Start cherishing. Make the change in your own life, and you'll be surprised what will happen in your husband's life.' This is straight out of the Bible. (Titus 2.)

"When your child falls down, you kiss the boo-boo and 'make it all better.' Mentors do the same. Like Ann, they calm and reassure you and take you to a still place. Whenever she calls on the telephone, I close the door and feast on her words of wisdom. As I tell my husband, 'What she imparts to me is like a box of Godiva chocolates. I'll never want a Hershey bar again!' When our third baby girl was born in 2000, John and I aptly named her Anna Elizabeth, a tribute to Ann Platz, a woman of great grace.'"

This darling daughter has learned well. When the day is done, is anyone going to recall the color of your dining room walls, or whether you were invited to the Swan Ball, or the amount of your stock portfolio? *God will be sizing up the way you honored and loved your husband and children and how you "kept" your home while marriages around you were crumbling.* It will be how you invested in eternal dividends. It will be how faithful you were in passing on the promises.

I learn from my mentorees too. Suzanne reminded me that the heart of the prayer of Jabez—the one Charlotte has prayed over me for the past eighteen years—is not that we may be blessed and "enlarged" for our own selfish gain, but that we may be blessed to be a blessing to others. We receive only that we may give. That's what mentoring is all about.

Victoria was another precious one whom I came to know a little later in her journey. She came to me quite by accident, at a book signing, after someone who had laid the foundations of her new faith had already mentored her. She opened up to me that day, and this is the story she shared with me.

Victoria's Secret

"I'm about what you could expect for a girl who grew up in a family of holiday Christians. You know, the ones who go to church on Easter and Christmas and rarely ever darken the door in between.

"I suppose things began to really go downhill for me when my sister died of cancer when I was fifteen. She was only thirteen years old. We had been cheerleaders, dancers, and gymnasts at school together. She was not only my sister—she was my friend. I was devastated.

"After she died, I began experimenting with alcohol. One night when I was so bombed I couldn't think straight, I was raped by a football player. When my grandfather died later that same year, I went off the deep end. By the time I was seventeen, I was pregnant, had had an abortion, and was totally out of control and into drugs and strip clubs.

"That's when I met Pam. Knowing I was dangerously suicidal, my live-in boyfriend, a drug dealer, asked her for help. She didn't offer any wise words or spout off Bible verses; she just handed him two tickets to the Singing Christmas Tree at her church. The real miracle is that we actually went!

"That night Pam had fifty people praying for the drug addict in the audience. They were praying for *me*. I remember thinking how pretty they all looked. Whole families sitting together. There were fathers and little girls.

"That was only the beginning. Even knowing who and what I was, Pam wouldn't let go of me. She called me constantly, even came to the house where I lived with the drug dealer, stepping over all the broken glass in the driveway.

"All this time she was telling me that no matter what I'd done or where I'd been, Jesus loves me just as I am. Six weeks later, at a Baptist church in a small Georgia town, I accepted Him as my Savior.

"I was still living with the drug dealer. Amazingly, Pam loved me through it all. Even when I was wearing tight jeans and low-cut blouses that were not very appropriate for this crowd, she would just put her arms around me and walk me into church.

"After I became a Christian, Steve was really upset and wanted me out of his house. When I left, I had nowhere to go but a local waffle house that was open all night. I sat there, reading my Bible and trying to pray. I heard a little voice saying, *Call the church,* so I did. I was told that Pam knew that Steve had kicked me out and wanted me to come live with her. I couldn't believe it! She had two little children and a husband—and she wanted *me?*

"Wow! When I saw the house, I realized that I'd really moved up in the world. Pam's husband had a great job with Georgia Power, and this was no shack. It was watching the family operate that really touched me. I'd had no idea before what a godly family was really like. They let me rest the first two weeks, just giving me some space and nurturing me back to health. Then Pam went through the clothes I'd brought in a garbage bag, weeded out the ones that smelled of pot, and suggested we go shopping. She taught me to cook, clean, and do simple chores around the house. Then, after a month, she helped me put together a résumé.

"Pam," I whined, "nobody's going to hire somebody like me." She sent me straight to the Word. "Trust God," she said. "He will provide," and He did! Not one, but two jobs!

"I won't say that I managed a clean pull off and was never tempted to go back to my old lifestyle. At one point I got bored with my telemarketing job, but Pam was there to encourage me and to keep me plugged in to the Lord. When I found Isaiah 43:18-20, it made all the difference: 'Forget all that [the old stuff]—it is nothing compared to what I'm going to do! For I'm going to do a brand new thing. See, I have already begun! Don't you see it? I will make a road through the wilderness of the world for my people to go home, and create rivers for them in the desert!...yes, springs in the desert, so that my people, my chosen ones, can be refreshed.' This was written for *me!*

"Believe me, the spiritual journey is anything but boring. As God opens your eyes to new revelation, He really does do new things. I married a wonderful Christian guy, and when we had our first child—a little boy—it finally dawned on me that I had murdered three babies (three abortions in the eleven years I had been on drugs). I joined a support group and mourned the loss of my children—even had a memorial for them. At that service, another Scripture was read that changed my life: 'Streams of tears flow from my eyes because my people are destroyed. My eyes will flow unceasingly, without relief, until the Lord looks down from heaven and sees. What I see brings grief to my soul because of all the women of my city'" (Lam. 3:48-51 NIV).

"That's when I began to understand that God had a real plan for my life. I was being sent back into the strip joints as a former stripper to witness to the girls hooked on sex and drugs. I don't mind telling you that I was terrified that first night. What if they chased me out? But just the opposite happened—they listened to my story. Within two months, twenty people called wanting to know more about Jesus! Three of them have been saved!

"Now we have kicked off a ministry called 'Victoria's Friends.' We are literally duplicating the mentoring relationship I formed with Pam, providing a way out of prostitution and connecting these girls with Christian families through the church. The mentor comes alongside for two or three months to show a girl her faith, befriend her, and plug her into the Lord.

"When I met Ann at a retreat where she was signing her book *The Best Is Yet to Come,* it had my name written all over it. The day of the luncheon was my fortieth birthday, so I bought her book as a gift to myself. For me, life really did begin at forty!

"One thing that Pam and Ann understand is that the church needs to embrace broken people, even 'garbage girls.' If the readers of this book—women of the church—don't take away anything else from my story, I really hope and pray that they get this:

> All you need to do is to stop oppressing the weak, and to stop making false accusations and spreading vicious rumors! Feed the hungry! Help those in trouble! Then your light will shine out from the darkness, and the darkness around you shall be as bright as day. And the Lord will guide you continually, and satisfy you with all good things, and keep you healthy too; and you will be like a well-watered garden, like an ever-flowing spring. Your sons will rebuild the long-deserted ruins of your cities, and you will be known as "The People Who Rebuild Their Walls and Cities."
>
> Isaiah 58:9-12

"I often wonder what I would have done if Pam hadn't taken a chance on me. A lot of good Christian people wouldn't take a risk like that, but it has been a double blessing for her to bless me and then to see the fruit.

"Now we're establishing a halfway house for these girls. Before they move in with a family, we screen the girls medically to reduce any possibility of spreading disease. A support group meets once a week, and we have big plans to tag-team with Teen Challenge and other ministries. We're looking for bold women—like Pam and Ann—who aren't afraid to love the unlovable."

I was so excited to hear Victoria's story and to have a part in reaching out to these precious young women. Her real life is just beginning.

Material Girl

At the other end of the social spectrum, Patty was reaching for the stars.

"From the time I was a little girl, I thought that if I could acquire just three things, I would be utterly and completely happy—a Cadillac, a diamond ring, and a full-length mink coat. So when I got them and I was not completely happy, I was disappointed and confused. Then God sent me Ann.

"We met while she was decorating a house I was renting. She would come in, take some measurements, arrange some furniture, and then leave an open Bible on the bookshelf. I would come behind her and close it, thinking she had mistakenly left it open. This happened several times, but I didn't think much about it.

"While she was decorating my house, she was really 'decorating my heart.' Before the project was finished, I was fascinated by her kindness, her sweetness, and her ability. In addition, I doubt that anyone could be around her long without being affected by her spiritually.

"Before long I was attending Bible studies and finding myself hungry for more. I prayed with Ann and Eliza to receive the Lord on the road between Atlanta and Athens, Georgia—where I had gone to hear Eliza speak. In the next few weeks, I was calling one or both of them two and three times a day. When a trip to the Holy Land was announced at a Bible study held at Dan and Eliza's, I asked Ann to go with me. Since I wanted to know everything I could learn about my newly discovered faith, in preparation for the trip, I read the entire Bible through in one month!

"It was on that trip to the Holy Land that Ann and John met and fell in love. God works in mysterious ways. I ended up being her maid of honor at a wedding where Ann—the expert on social graces—broke the old rule that bridesmaids have to pay a fortune for a dress they will wear once, then hang in the back of the closet. Instead, she asked us to wear our prettiest spring dresses. The wedding was perfectly beautiful. The pastels blended like spring flowers, and everyone took note of the bride's thoughtfulness.

"I guess I didn't realize that most new Christians don't have such spiritual giants to jump-start their walk with the Lord. I just loved being around them. I tried to soak in everything they taught me— from the social graces to how to handle difficult life situations.

"Ann once pointed out to me that *every human being—even Christians—will disappoint you at one time or another,* but that I shouldn't let that discourage me. It's only part of their humanity. I have passed on that important truth to many Christians. It helps us not to give up on people.

"That's what mentors do. They never give up on their children...."

When Patty is ready to reproduce spiritually, I can't wait to see what those children will look like! They will have their mother's enthusiasm, joy, and increasing wisdom—and their Father's strength. They will be my grandchildren, and I will enjoy being a part of their lives. Since God saw fit to send Patty two mentors at one time, I suspect He is entrusting her with a double measure of responsibility and blessing. She will measure up. She's my girl!

The Lyon Roars

And then there is Dee. I have not known this precious woman as long as some of my own spiritual daughters, but her story could have been a rerun of Victoria's—*if it had not been for an understanding mentor!*

Dee describes her early years as a Christian and her divine encounter with Fran: "I proudly exited the church aisle to head for my first bona fide communion. I remember my outfit clearly. The blouse was fire engine red with a matching red-checked micro-mini skirt and excessively high-heeled boots, which caused me to walk with a stumbling gait. I was a new Christian at the time, so full of excitement about the experience of feeling God's presence that I was unaware of the raised eyebrows in the congregation when they saw what I considered haute couture.

"It was difficult to find a mentor who was not embarrassed to be with me during that stage of my life. That changed when I met Fran. She never mentioned my appearance, my behavior, or my need to change. She merely taught me the Scriptures, helped me memorize them, and continually encouraged me to 'trust and obey.' Fran even helped me, skimpy sundresses and all, with administrative tasks in some of her evangelistic meetings and, in so doing, helped me feel a part of the body of Christ.

"When my husband died of cancer, I could hear Fran saying, 'As for God, His way is perfect' (Ps. 18:30 NKJV).

"When I was diagnosed with a life-threatening illness and was placed in the intensive care unit thirty times, I heard her say, 'Bless the Lord...who forgives all your iniquities, who heals all your diseases' (Ps. 103:2,3 NKJV).

"When people are in trouble or ill, I hear her tell me, 'Bear one another's burdens, and so fulfill the law of Christ' (Gal. 6:2 NKJV).

"All of the Scriptures that Fran encouraged me to memorize were there at the forefront of my mind when I needed one of God's promises for my own life or when I needed to share with others. I spent five years under Fran's patient tutelage and have benefited for the last thirty years. Had someone else tried to mentor me—someone who pointed out all the 'you should nots'—I would have missed the unconditional love of God and His promise to mature a seeking heart."

My Cup of Joy Is Full

When I consider my progeny—all the spiritual daughters and granddaughters the Lord has given me—I see a banquet table set with fine china and sparkling silver. We are ready to partake of the feast He has prepared for us. As I look from one beloved face to the other, my heart swells with love and gratitude. What I have given has been returned a hundredfold, pressed down and overflowing. My cup of joy is full!

CHAPTER 15

The Impartation

I long to see you, that I may impart to you some spiritual gift,
so that you may be established—that is, that I may be
encouraged together with you by [our] mutual faith.

ROMANS 1:11

As I sit in my cozy corner at the mountain house, rereading the pages of this manuscript as it flows from His heart through the precious women He has placed in my life, I am weeping. Once again, I am overwhelmed by the way in which He intervenes in our lives. To take women, warts and all, and allow us to participate in kingdom enterprises is a merciful act that takes my breath away.

Rather than being puffed up by the sweet words of my mentorees, I am challenged to stay alert to every opportunity to extend God's love and kindness. I don't want to miss anything—or anyone—the Lord has for me.

Too, *it is fascinating to see how He continues to weave a rich tapestry of life, created by the many patterns of personality and gifting that each mentor and mentoree represent.* Together we are becoming a work of great beauty and infinite worth for His glory.

Of all my mentors—each one a powerful woman of God—Doris Crenshaw is the one He placed in my life to launch me into the next level of my deeper walk with Him. I'll never forget the weekend I received an impartation from her that would change my ministry.

Lioness for the Lord

Our mountain house can easily accommodate sixteen people overnight, and we adore entertaining—particularly when we are working from the Lord's agenda. Several times I have prayed that He would prepare an invitation list and allow me to host just the mix of people to whom He would like to give some special blessing. As a result, we have had some spectacular events. When these gatherings of "eagles" occur, the anointing and impartation are so profound that the ladies can almost literally fly off that mountaintop on the way home.

One such fall weekend brought me the surprise of my life. The color that year was glorious—brilliant yellows and fiery reds, a flaming promise of all that was to come. The ladies—a cross-section of old friends and new acquaintances—had thoroughly enjoyed the days spent together in prayer and Bible study, and we were finding it difficult to leave after our Sunday brunch. There were plenty of tears as the cars were loaded for the ride down the mountain.

About that time, Doris tapped me on the shoulder and said, "I need you out on the screened porch, Ann. We're going to have a deliverance."

Doris is one of the women I most admire in the world. If she had asked me to prepare myself for execution, I would have trusted her to pull something off at the last minute. As it was, I dutifully hugged the last of my guests and reported to the porch as directed.

Among the few guests remaining was a dear friend who had experienced great loss early in life with the death of both parents. As a result, fear had taken up residence in her spirit, and the door was open for the enemy to come in and harass her. She was sick and tired of it, and ready to be rid of that fear.

I had already felt the Lord's calm presence earlier—a kind of knowing that He was going to show me deep and wondrous things. Simultaneously, there was a tingling in my inner being. I forgot everything else and concentrated. I was certain that whatever came next would be powerful. Little did I know, however, that the Lord had something for *me*.

Actually, in the beginning, my friend was hesitant about opening up. She had some tender, private issues that she was ashamed for me to hear, concerned that I might be disappointed in her, but she graciously agreed for me to stay. As Doris says, "Honey, you haven't got a single sin I haven't heard before." Besides, I was not there to gather gossip. I was there to learn from a great mentor.

Even though Doris, a striking brunette, is a dainty woman, she can roar like a lion when she is engaging the enemy in combat. She took the full authority given her in Christ and commanded the spirit of fear to come out. (Luke 10:19; Heb. 2). I was wide-eyed—like the art student who is holding the scaffolding for the master painter—taking in every word she said. Doris would issue a command, and then ask my friend what she was feeling. My friend continued to feel panicky and fearful. Doris regrouped and issued the command once more: "One, two, three," she counted. "Come out of her in the name of Jesus Christ!"

Having been present to experience deliverance before, I knew that some demons manifest themselves in fits of coughing or gagging or in any number of ways, but this was a first. My friend's eyes literally bulged like fish eyes! Immediately thereafter, she cried, "It's gone!"

If I hadn't been there, I might have doubted this story. God knows that I am a literal and pragmatic person. He knows that I will follow Him anywhere when I'm sure He is leading. This was totally God. I experienced the same sensation I had felt the night Mary Crum first prophesied over me; the first time Eliza said, "There's so much more for you." This moment was linked with the others in the same degree of certainty and assurance. The providential hand of God was all over it. My friend was completely set free that day, never to suffer a minute of depression again!

At that point Doris turned around and fixed her piercing gaze on me. "You've got to know how to do this to be effective in the ministry God has called you to." I knew she was right. I had reached the next level, the next impartation. The Lord showed me immediately that deliverance would be a part of my future ministry. I don't have a Ph.D. in deliverance. All I can say is that God did it, I saw it, and now I believe.

Only He could know that less than two months later, I would require this training to prepare me for another crisis. I was on high alert.

Daughter of Deliverance

Doris Crenshaw was launched into ministry, along with Mary Crum, when they attended a meeting under a prophetic move of God that had broken loose in Florida. The impartation that Bishop Hamon gave that weekend released both women, like Isaiah and Jeremiah, to speak healing and deliverance to the nations.

Doris explains a variety of ways in which impartation takes place.

Laying on of Hands

There is something mysterious and powerful in the human touch. Under the anointing of the Holy Spirit and in obedience to the Word of God (Acts 8:17), you are in a divine partnership that breaks strongholds and releases healing.

The Presence of Power

Sometimes simply being in the presence of an anointed servant of God imparts a blessing that defies description. When some people have come into our home, which is designed to provide comfort and sanctuary for the spirit, they have told me they leave with something they didn't expect to receive.

Mentors will impart the level of their anointing to you. It is also possible to receive an unholy impartation. Checking the credibility of the source will protect you from this danger. That is why it is imperative that in these days of mass-media communication, we guard our minds with all diligence. Be careful what you see—allow to enter through the eye-gates—and what you hear—allow to enter through the ear-gates. You absorb more than you realize, and that "impartation" lingers long.

As a younger woman, fresh from a painful divorce, part of the impartation I received from Eliza and Dan was in the area of marriage. I observed how much they loved each other, how they served and ministered to each other. It was refreshing to see the example of a godly marriage. John and I "caught" that impartation, and we pass it on in our own ministry. Both of my daughters and all of my spiritual daughters look to John as the model of a godly husband and father.

Anointing With Oil

The anointing oil used in Bible days was usually olive oil and was applied to the forehead or head of the recipient. Anointing with oil, which represents the Holy Spirit, is a physical impartation with spiritual results. When we obey His direct instructions (Matt. 6:17; James 5:14,15), whether we understand them or not, we will reap enormous benefits.

Igniting the Gift

The mentor with the discernment to see your spiritual gifts is also the one who strikes the match to ignite those gifts. She cannot call forth what isn't there, but she can stir up what is already within you, just waiting to burst into bloom.

Lifting the Veil

On her wedding day, a bride is usually veiled. This is a tradition that symbolizes purity and chastity. However, the veil also obscures vision. When the veil is lifted, not only can you see your true love, but also you can see your destiny and will be able to march toward it with eyes sparkling and step eager. From the mentor will come an impartation to pursue that destiny that will set you free from past chains of bondage.

Doris was once invited by the pastor of a mainline denominational church to speak to his congregation in a small town in South Carolina. The church had been struggling, with only 100 or so in attendance on the first night of the event. Hoping to bring some light and hope to the people, Doris asked the pastor what he perceived to be the biggest hindrance to the growth of the church. "The spirit of lust," he replied, adding that he meant greed, materialism, power, sex, and all its many faces.

With that in mind, Doris decided to begin with a mass deliverance so that the people would be able to receive the Word of God. Getting right to the point, she said, "In the name of Jesus, I call out the spirit of lust in this body!" Practically everyone in the entire congregation began throwing up! Someone ran for paper towels. All of the elders were gagging and coughing. Even the pastor's wife ran out of the church. This went on for an hour or so. The next night the church was packed. The news of a major revival had spread all over town!

What Doris didn't know was the history of that church. The pastor had sadly disappointed his congregation by engaging in serious unethical conduct, including suspected criminal activity.

The Mantle Falls

To *impart* is "to convey, to grant, to confer, to place upon another person—as with a lovely shawl or cloak—a body of knowledge or wisdom drawn from a deep well of experience." When we impart to others something that we know or have experienced, we are giving them a portion of ourselves. More importantly, we are granting them a measure of God's Spirit, who indwells us.

Each mentor comes with a unique impartation. God has used my giftings in the areas of art and design to impart excellence and transformation. I absolutely love seeing a house—or a life—move into a radical new dimension. Doris imparts deliverance. Mary Crum operates in the prophetic. The two women remind me of salt and pepper—together, they represent the perfect seasoning for the "meal." There are times when the impartations and the giftings overlap and under-line each other. At those times our ministries are all increased and brought into a more perfect harmony and balance.

Not only have we been woven together spiritually but also, to our surprise, Mary Crum and I found that we both share the same silver pattern with Doris, who is now beginning her collection. There are more accessory pieces in this pattern than any other—ice tongs, pickle forks, grapefruit spoons, ice cream spoons—for the woman who loves to serve and is planning a smorgasbord of delicacies to meet every need of her guests, but it is the knives are that are the most significant to us. On the handle are twenty-eight fruits—the signature of the Spirit.

Through the impartations given to me by Doris and Mary and the anointing of the Holy Spirit, I am better equipped to meet needs on many levels. As I speak and conduct seminars, or greet people at book signings, I can now more quickly discern a stronghold that requires deliverance or an unspoken heartache that needs healing. The Spirit often gives me a word of prophecy or knowledge that sends someone on her way in a new direction. "Preach the Word of God urgently at all times whenever you get the chance, in season and out, when it is convenient and when it is not" (2 Tim. 4:2).

Therefore, I was alert and prepared when a friend called in great distress some time after our mountain retreat. Her doctor had given her a grim diagnosis for the symptoms she described—either multi-ple sclerosis or chronic fatigue syndrome. I called Doris immediately and asked if this case might be handled through deliverance. She assured me that it could be. I set up a session for my very willing friend and this time participated with Doris. The heart of the matter was indeed spiritual—my friend had never received Jesus as her

Savior. By the third session, we prayed for her to receive the Lord, and healing and deliverance came!

Some question the reality of such healings, believing that they are brought about by the power of suggestion. Pat Robertson writes:

It is possible that some people are healed of psychosomatic illnesses by suggestion. There are many examples of healings that could not be explained in these terms. Here is just one.

At age nineteen, Barbara Cummiskey was diagnosed as having multiple sclerosis. By the time she was thirty-one, the multiple sclerosis had helped cause a slowly paralyzing diaphragm, bouts of pneumonia and asthma, a collapsed lung, and tumors on her hands. She was technically blind and confined to her bed. There were well-diagnosed medical problems, and she was operated on more than once. But on June 7, 1981, she heard a voice say, "My child, get up and walk." She did just that and was healed! Barbara's legs had atrophied from lack of exercise. When she first got out of bed, however, her legs had muscle tone. Her mother shouted, "Calves! You have calves!"

Similarly, I have come across instances where people were not near a television set when *The 700 Club* was used by God to heal them. One man went to bed blind, but a prayer request came in to our television program for him, and when he woke up, he could see.[1]

I don't know how God works in the supernatural. We don't have to know everything. I only know that He is the same God He has always been; He never changes. And I know that He has told me not to be afraid of the miraculous. Although I am not an ordained minister, I am called of God to help deliver His people. I accept that calling

with the utmost humility and with gratitude to the precious women—
and men—who led me into that calling.

I am Doris's and Mary's spiritual daughter. I am Daddy's daughter. I am my heavenly Father's daughter, and the mantle has fallen.

THE KINGDOM GATES:
YOUR GOLDEN FUTURE

So, dear [sisters], work hard to prove

that you really are among those God

has called and chosen.

And God will open wide the gates of heaven

for you to enter into the eternal kingdom

of our Lord and Savior Jesus Christ.

2 PETER 1:10,11

Queen Esther

Esther, the Old Testament beauty contestant who won a crown and a kingdom, has always been one of my heroines. She teaches us that physical beauty is bestowed for a purpose, not for personal gain.

Yet, Esther would never have become queen without the patient instruction of her mentor, her Uncle Mordecai. As she endured the yearlong ritual of beauty preparations—the finest oils and lotions and perfumes—her uncle was preparing her heart to remember the faith of her fathers and from whence she had come.

Later, when wicked Haman conceived a plot to destroy the Jews, her uncle encouraged her to be courageous, for "who knows whether you have come to the kingdom for such a time as this?" (Est. 4:14 NKJV). Upon her slender shoulders rested the fate of a nation!

When she was at last presented to the king, he found her lovelier—perhaps because of that inner glow—than all the other fair maidens of the land, and placed the crown on her head. In due time, she would approach him in behalf of her people, and he would grant her petition.

Mentors prepare us for an audience with the King!

CHAPTER 16

Lifeline to Your Destiny

*Two can accomplish more than twice as much
as one, for the results can be much better....
One standing alone can be attacked and defeated, but two
can stand back-to-back and conquer; three is even better,
for a triple-braided cord is not easily broken.*

ECCLESIASTES 4:9,12

Being my mother's daughter, I have always loved company. Entertaining, for me, as it is for her, is second nature—whether it's coffee with a friend or the most elaborate dinner party. I'm happiest when there are lots of people around—especially my family.

In my profession, as well, people are important. With my years of training and experience in the field of interior design, I so enjoy working with others whose area of expertise complements my own. From the architect to the landscape designer, when we pool our talents and gifts, the result is far greater than any of us could achieve alone. I am a team player.

In the same way, when the Spirit of God links mentors and mentorees, both are blessed with fruitfulness that reaches to the uttermost parts of the earth. As my friend Lizanne says, any Christian relationship enriches her life, but the mentoring relationship is the highest form of friendship. We need someone to walk with us, to interpret some spiritual truth we might otherwise miss, to impart wisdom, to be a lifeline to heaven.

The Holy Spirit, the ultimate mentor, often deposits people at our doorstep, people who have lost their way and need a roadmap. Jody was one of those.

Road Map to Heaven

In walking together, the mentor must be available and the mentoree must be authentic. She cannot keep secrets or hide the painful past.

Jody was honest and candid, ready to share a long litany of woes: an abused childhood; the traumatic death of a parent; financial reversals—from posh private school to supporting herself at the age of sixteen; emotional damage—marriage and betrayal by the husband she trusted. She was on the high wire with no safety net. She couldn't afford to make too many mistakes, but the hits continued.

Both of her sons were involved in car accidents within two or three years, resulting in staggering medical bills. Her house burned down, and the rental house they moved into was struck by lightning. You guessed it—she had no insurance. Most people would have buckled under such intense attack, but Jody's children were watching. She braced herself to be strong for them.

That's when God brought Linda and me into Jody's life. I modeled one kind of spiritual profile for her. Linda, with her background of singleness, was able to pass on to Jody what she had gleaned from me.

Jody lives with her boss and his wife, for whom she has worked for some time. This gracious southern couple is deeply rooted in the community. As Jody began to be transformed before their very eyes, the difference was so striking that they began to comment on the changes. The wife even asked Jody one day, "Is there a new man in your life?" Jody only smiled, thinking how surprised they would be to hear about the new Man in her life!

"God has brought me a beautiful bouquet of women mentors," Jody told my editor in a recent interview. "In Ann, I saw a woman who excelled in many areas—marriage, motherhood, business—a woman of God. In her, I was seeing that you _can_ have it all if you know how to prioritize your relationship with God and others. In Linda, I was learning to trust Him for all the 'impossibles' in my life. It was like opening the door to a secret garden and finding great beauty, peace, and joy, and the fragrance of lives lived well for Christ. I wanted that too."

Jody was a quick study. Coming from a religious background, she had not really embraced all that Jesus had to offer her until our association with her. After soaking up everything we had to suggest, she was now drawing other women to her like bees to honey.

One of those "bees" was a ninety-four-year-old Swedish woman who lives in a small seaside community where Jody visits with her employers. Brilliant and youthful, Estelle pedals her three-wheel bicycle like a fifty-year-old and demonstrates her zest for living in ways that endear her to everyone she meets. She and Jody were drawn to each other.

As Jody opened up, sharing her new life in the Spirit, Estelle seemed hungry to know more. Jody obliged with books and tapes. One afternoon they were watching a video from a large Spirit-filled church in Florida when the pastor closed the program with an invitation. "Any of you—here in the church or watching us on television—raise your hands if you wish to have prayer to receive the baptism of the Holy Spirit." To Jody's utter amazement, Estelle's crippled, wrinkled hands shot up.

In a recent e-mail, Jody explains what happened next. "As I laid my hands on her and prayed, Ann, God gave this woman the baptism of the Holy Spirit. Oh, it was real...believe me, it was real: her expression, watching, as she looked at her own body to see the Spirit come upon her. It was the presence of the Lord! But that isn't the end of the story.

"Estelle had packed her nightgown in a bag and brought it along. She said this was something she had never done before, and she didn't know how to explain it, except that 'something' had told her to stay with me.

"The next morning we attended church together, and I was thanking and praising God for what He had done for her when He said—and this is as clear as it gets, Ann—*Jody, this was your first lamb, one that I especially chose to give you. You are a good shepherd.*"

Jody can't wait to see what develops next!

Timeline to Eternity

Time is such a precious commodity. We often joke about its passing, saying things like "Time flies when you're having fun!" But the truth is that, by earthly standards, there is only so much of it, and it is quickly running out. As in the lives of the two ladies at my dinner party, in each life will come moments of discovery that may never come again. We can waste time; or we can make the most of it, seizing those seasons of eternal significance.

At birth, every person is given a number of days known only to the Father. At that moment the countdown to the end of earthly existence begins. We are accountable to God for the way in which we spend our days.

When your mentors move into place to nurture your life, they will open up a whole new dimension of God's custom-tailored timeline for your destiny. You will begin to measure your days by His yardstick: What are the plans He has for you to accomplish while you are here? Some of the causes and activities to which you devote so much time and energy will be as useless and meaningless as chaff, the dry, empty husks of wheat that, in biblical times, were burned after the harvest. (Matt. 3:12.) Better be sure that your deeds are rich and full of life so that you will emerge from the fires of testing as pure gold.

In these days we are moving so close to the fulfillment of prophecy. Jesus' return could very easily be within our lifetime; but even if it is not, we will see Him soon—one way or another. John's closest friend, Ray, a man thirteen years younger, had been in excellent health until he was recently diagnosed with leukemia and died three weeks later! We don't have the promise of tomorrow, only today.

While I'm not worried about the end of life, I believe we should be living every day as if it might be the last. As a wonderful woman named Peggy, who teaches at the Life Center, said just the other day: "God is the eternal I Am. If you are His child, you are always in the I Am mode. Every moment with the Lord is fresh and new as He intersects your life and connects you with others in His kingdom plan. Therefore, it isn't necessary to be concerned about where you need to be, or when you need to get there, or what you should be doing. *It's a now faith, and every moment is ripe with promise!"*

Peggy is so right. Every moment is precious.

The Refreshing

Have you ever had a day when you'd been at some all-day meeting or running the carpool or supervising a fifth-grade field trip, and all you wanted to do when you got home was to throw your things down on the nearest chair and fall into bed? That's the way I sometimes feel spiritually when I've spent myself in ministry, giving and imparting, and needing to be refilled. It's a place the Lord loves to meet me. There, in the stillness, I can hear Him whisper, "My grace is sufficient for you, for My strength is made perfect in weakness" (2 Cor. 12:9 NKJV).

I love to bathe in His Word, meditating on it, letting it become alive in me. I want to experience it, to dance before the Lord, to move into worship, to let my spirit be saturated with the truth and the life of God. I want more of Him, more of His fullness, everything He has for me!

As a history major in college, I loved to read and research all the great historical eras, so even those detailed accounts in Kings and Chronicles sound like music to my ears. But more than that, when the Holy Spirit ignites the Word, it literally dances off the pages.

In the presence of the Lord, I find complete and utter fulfillment. It is better than the grandest tourist attractions of the world—the view from the top of the Eiffel Tower in Paris, the skyline of Rome at night from the rooftop of the Hassler Hotel, the breathtaking vista of the city of Jerusalem as seen from the Mount of Olives. It is not a geographical location. It is a location of the heart.

Once, while sitting in church during the sermon after a powerful praise and worship service, I felt that I had almost entered the Holy of Holies. The air got very still. Something changed in the atmosphere, and I could see a thin vapor starting at the top of the sanctuary.

In that supercharged moment, there was a sense that everything had ceased to exist except God. It was a holy moment, a stillness of awe.

A good mentor makes her mentorees aware that such experiences are real and that they can expect them. All my children are hyperactive—jumpin', joyful daughters of the Lord. I just tell them to expect more and more as they grow and increase and move from "glory to glory." (2 Cor. 3:18.) I fully anticipate that they will far surpass me in their spiritual exploits, and I love it!

My natural daughters, Margo and Courtney, who have inherited a legacy of love and instruction from me as their mother, also have some of my spiritual traits and impartations. In the dispensation of time, they will likely be nearer the return of the Lord than I. Therefore; their ministries will be even more powerful. That's as it should be. I don't want any of my daughters sitting around filing their nails. I want them to be about their Father's business. Time's a-wastin'!

A Bertie in the Hand

My friend Martha is a darling mutual mentor whom I adore. When I need a deposit from the mother lode of righteousness, Martha imparts to me. When she needs a tweaking of truth, I impart to her. It is a rich, rewarding relationship.

A mentor of hers was Bertie Webb. Several others in this book gleaned from her too. Martha likes to share what this woman meant to her.

"There was no way of knowing that day I walked out of Emory Hospital that one of the dearest friends a human being can have could be taken from this earth in a matter of two days. She was being sent home to die. She told me so. The doctors had given her two weeks to live.

"As I walked out of the hospital, a blast of August heat hit me in the face. My heart was wrenched in pain. Somewhat dazed, I had to focus to recall exactly where my car was parked. Finding the car, I buckled my seat belt, my Sunday dress clinging to my skin. Driving home, I felt a foreboding sense that my life was about to change drastically.

"In the five years since the death of Bertie Webb, the memories of the golden deposits she put within my life come to mind regularly. She was not only a friend extraordinaire but also a mentor whose life lessons are bringing transformation within me even now.

"Bertie was a dispenser of wisdom, which she gleaned from reading the Bible, keeping company with the wise, and learning well the lessons life taught her. In order to absorb wisdom, it is absolutely necessary to keep company with the wise. 'He who walks [as a companion] with wise men shall be wise' (Prov. 14:21 AMP).

"One could beat every bush on the planet and not find a duplicate of Bertie. She took me from crayons to perfume in the ministry. How blessed I am, indeed, to have walked a portion of my Christian journey with my mentor, Bertie, for an all-too-brief season. She gave me so much that she left me full to overflowing. It was that way the day she died. It is that way today.

"If you are fortunate enough to have a 'Bertie' in your life, cherish her and hold on to her for as long as the Lord allows. People like her do not come along very often. From the time Bertie died, I have always said, 'A Bertie in the hand is worth two in the bush.'"

I knew and loved Bertie, too. From Martha, who learned it from Bertie, I have discovered how to find peace in green pastures, how to set boundaries, and how to laugh at myself when life is too intense. On our journey to eternity, we must clasp our friends and mentors to our hearts, learn their secrets, and pass on their wisdom to the next generation.

CHAPTER 17

Passing the Torch

Whatever happens, dear friends, be glad in
the Lord. I never get tired of telling you this....
All these things that I once thought very
worthwhile—now I've thrown them all away so
that I can put my trust and hope in Christ alone....
I strain to reach the end of the race and
receive the prize for which God is calling us.

PHILIPPIANS 3:1,7,14

Trust me. I am no athlete. Sports are not my cup of tea. The nearest I ever get to a ballgame or a track meet is when I'm flipping the channels on TV looking for a good program to watch.

So when my cousin Betsy called with a suggestion that we join her at the Summer Olympics the year they were held in Atlanta, I all but politely declined. John and I had made plans to head for our mountain retreat to escape the sweltering heat and the record crowds projected to descend on the city. If Betsy and her husband, Dick, hadn't been our favorite cousins...

Needless to say, we capitulated and found ourselves among the throngs gazing in awe at the unfolding events of the opening ceremonies: the colorful parade of nations; the athletes dressed in native attire, bearing their countries' flags; the moving speeches; the inspired music; the fanfare of trumpets; the spectacular fireworks; and finally, the lighting of the sacred fire, signaling the beginning of the Games.

The history buff that I am, I had done my homework and learned that the event had its origins in Greece in 776 BC. The original flame—a symbol of the spirit, knowledge, and life of the world's nations—is alleged to have been ignited by the rays of the sun in Olympia. Today, the Olympic torch is lighted four weeks prior to the games. Runners, from Olympia to the host city, then relay the flame. Once the flame arrives, it is used to light the Olympic stadium cauldron, which burns throughout the Games.

What a perfect portrait of the mentoring relationship. One runner, the mentor, receives the torch from another and passes it on!

Surprisingly, the games themselves also intrigued me. I will never throw a javelin or run a marathon, but that week I observed the best of the best athletes in competition, using every bit of their training and gifting. It was the experience of a lifetime to watch these athletes performing with such precision and excellence. John, sitting beside me, explained each contest as it was introduced. I drank it all in, energized and inspired by this display of the versatility and power of the human body.

If we can receive inspiration from watching a sports activity, just think what the power of the Holy Spirit can do in a learning experience with Him! When you have an opportunity to sit at the feet of the best—whether human or divine—don't decline the invitation. Be there!

The Eternal Flame

The lighting of the Olympic fire is admittedly a pagan ritual, dedicated to Greek gods and goddesses. But I can't help thinking how we, as believers in the only true God, have the opportunity to take back what has been stolen from us and championed by the world. He who is the light of the world, the only Son of God, is the source of all truth and knowledge. As we learn from Him, either directly or through the mentors He sends our way, He ignites our spirits with a flame that will burn eternally. When it is time, we hand on this wisdom and truth to the next person, until all the generations have heard. "One generation shall praise Your works to another, and shall declare Your mighty acts" (Ps. 145:4). Our testimony is the torch God uses to light the way to eternity.

One whose flame burns brightly is Kay, a precious friend. Kay is a doll. Five foot, two inches tall, she is a platinum blond with enormous, china-blue eyes. She is also a publicist—the one who happened to be assigned to one of my first books, *A Match Made in Heaven.*

It was her bright idea to stage a book promotion with an upscale jewelry store on Valentine's Day and offer an autographed copy of the book, instructing readers to read a true love story every night to their spouses. The event, coordinated with a radio station in town, was wildly successful. Caught up in the mood of the moment, the owners of the store, a couple who had been taking ballroom dancing lessons, encouraged their customers to dance with them right in the store! It was fresh and spontaneous and joyful, a work of the Spirit in an otherwise secular environment. Everyone had a ball!

Kay had been one of my mentorees when she'd lived in Atlanta, a season of her life when she says she didn't have any friends. She was hungry for a hero, someone to idolize. Actually, she was hungry for

God and didn't know it. So I filled her in. "Kay, you have to live life like a trapeze artist. Have the faith to let go. Be prepared to change direction when the Spirit nudges you. But don't be afraid when God takes you to the next level of maturity and you find yourself on the bottom rung of the ladder again. That just means He is seriously accelerating your growth. You've got to learn His patterns and the way He does things—even if it's a little uncomfortable for you."

That's how she felt professionally, she says, when she ended up in Dallas—"uncomfortable, unsure, shaky." But that's when she developed the spiritual muscle to go the distance. When she was on her own with the Lord, not so dependent on a physical mentor, she learned to lean on Him, and her spiritual life took off along with her business. She also learned that when God gives you a mentor, He expects you to *become* a mentor—to pass the torch to the next hungry heart. "If you have a Paul in your life," she says, "there will also eventually be a Timothy." Look for the one God is positioning to receive an impartation from you.

Kay began her own work as a mentor by "taking the torch" to Dallas. Now, through the media, she is busily promoting kingdom work with an impact that is quite literally felt around the world. Meanwhile, closer to home, she illuminates the darkness for troubled boys, serving as a volunteer in a home for juvenile delinquents. Her flame—God's truth and beauty reflected in her—is lighting their way home.

Interestingly enough, she has mentored me in a roundabout sort of way. By helping publicize the books I write to the glory of God, she is spreading the Word. Each time we hold a book promotion, we are fulfilling the Great Commission: "Go and make disciples in all the nations, baptizing them into the name of the Father and of the Son and of the Holy Spirit, and then teach these new disciples to obey all the commands I have given you" (Matt. 28:19,20).

Pass It On

It was while signing books one summer at CBA—Christian Booksellers Association's annual conference—that I first realized that a prophecy spoken over me was being fulfilled at that very moment. One by one, as the conference-goers stepped up to my table with a book to be signed, I got a glimpse of what God was doing. Standing in line was someone from Japan, a woman from England, a couple from France, a Filipino—each of them a reader of one or more of my books who had been touched or changed in some way. God was showing me how He was increasing distribution—more widely than any marketing division or book publisher in the world—and producing transformation through the printed word.

It is a mystery how words and ideas can travel so far. Like the wind, like the oceans that begin as small streams and widen into many waters, so the concept of God's infinite love moves by way of His messengers. One by one, we hand off what we have gained through years of intimacy with God and through contact with those who model the essence of truth.

Sometimes the handoff is not smooth, and there are pebbles on the path. One such "glitch" was the time Eliza and I were mentoring a dear daughter who, as an unbeliever, was seeing a married man. Once she came to the Lord, we encouraged her to give up her ungodly lifestyle and set the bar higher. The man she had been seeing, a prominent citizen of the community, called in the Georgia Bureau of Investigation to do a background check on the two meddling mentors. At this point in this story, Eliza would be telling me, "Tell 'em what the report said." So I will. The official report of the GBI lists Eliza and me as "Fine people, but a little too religious." If you ask me, that's a good report!

The mentoree asked the Lord to forgive her, put the affair behind her, and has gone on to marry and grow strong in the Lord. His power—imparted through two very human mentors—has proven greater than the influence of the married man and the Georgia Bureau of Investigation combined!

Each person has been given gifts, not to be squandered on selfish pursuits, but to bless the whole body.

God has given each of you some special abilities; be sure to use them to help each other, passing on to others God's many kinds of blessings. Are you called to preach? Then preach as though God himself were speaking through you. Are you called to help others? Do it with all the strength and energy that God supplies, so that God will be glorified through Jesus Christ—to him be glory and power forever and ever.

1 Peter 4:10,11

Or, as Eliza says, "Pass it on."

The Torchbearers

All of us—spiritual mentors and mentorees alike—are torchbearers. The question is whether our flames are hot and bright or dim and flickering. Either way, we must never let the flame go out. Even on our worst days, when everything seems to be going wrong, we need to hang on to the sure Word of God and the witness of others. That is one reason for the birth of this book: to encourage my daughters in the Lord to press on and pass the torch.

Sometimes, though, in God's scheme of things, a torchbearer is advancing the flame most effectively while running in place. One runner named Brenda, who holds her torch high, is spending this season caring for her invalid mother in her home.

What brought Brenda to this place of servanthood and sainthood reads like an epic novel: The "perfect" marriage, blessed with a daughter, was ripped apart by her husband's infidelity and deception. This left Brenda's identity and future in limbo for months, leading to a complete nervous breakdown. Her mother arrived to celebrate what would have been an otherwise bleak Christmas, suffered a stroke, and never returned to her own home.

During this time, God used many precious people, including lifelong friends, to bring Brenda back to full health and to help her find her identity as a woman of God. For eleven years now, Brenda's torch, while flickering at times, has provided light for her small family and the fortunate others who cross her path to bask in the warmth for a short season or an eternal friendship.

She was nearly shipwrecked when John and I found her, washed up on the shores of my interior design firm, needing a job. The Holy Spirit made it very clear that we were to take her under our wing. We obeyed and set about to repair the damages and help Brenda stage a comeback. With love and much prayer, her latent abilities began to shine, and she eventually became our marketing director. This position eventually led to the formation of her own company when the mentoring season was over.

"Before my divorce, I trusted the Lord to get me to heaven," Brenda explains, "but I didn't trust Him to get me across the street. Now my Lord and Savior, the ultimate mentor, is my everything—my husband, my provider, my mother (when she is too ill to communicate), my Father, my friend. There is nothing I have ever needed that He has not provided."

Some think Brenda's sacrifice in caring for her mother is noble. Brenda considers it an honor and a privilege. "There is a song that speaks of the cycle of life," she recalls. "As an infant is utterly dependent upon the mother for food and nurture—'You are my eyes, my hands, my arms, my feet'—there will come a time when the role is reversed, and the daughter becomes the mother's eyes and hands and arms and feet. That's how it is for Mother and me now. Even on those days, though, I'm still my mother's little girl.

"At the end of a long day I will slip downstairs to her room, find her sitting in her chair by the window, and lay my head in her lap while she strokes my hair. When the Lord finally takes her home, I'll miss her, but I'll be okay. From her, from other mentors, and from Jesus Christ, I have learned to be better, not bitter, when life hands me a curveball.

"Recently, while walking on the beach with my own married daughter during a rare retreat from my caretaker role, we fell into deep conversation. 'Mama,' she began a little pensively, 'when I have children someday, what is the one piece of advice you would give me as a parent?'

"I had opened my mouth to tell her it would be to lead her child to the Lord at an early age, when she stopped me. 'But, Mom, not the God stuff. I already know what you would say about that!'

"I chuckled, thinking how well she knew my heart, just as I now know my Father's heart and have come to trust Him in every tiny aspect of my life. 'Well, then,' I replied, 'I would say that the most important thing to teach your child is that he or she should never, ever doubt that you would be there to listen, to advise, to encourage; that no matter what, your love is unconditional.'"

At that moment I believe Brenda's flame blazed more brightly than ever, lighting the way for generations yet unborn.

A Journey With a Wise Friend

Lizanne describes the mentoring relationship as a journey with a wise friend. In the beginning, the relationship is at one level. Much like a marathon race, as the journey continues, the surroundings change. Along the way there are beautiful vistas, hilly terrain, and high hurdles. The runner's physical body must be maintained, with rest stops and time for refreshing. The weight of excess baggage from the past must be unloaded.

Like sheep, we are not to bear heavy loads. Sheep are not burden-bearing beasts but are followers, intended to trail behind the shepherd, the mentor, who leads them into green pastures and beside still waters and satisfies their hunger and thirst. Where they will eventually end up—or when—is insignificant.

Like impatient children headed for a vacation at the beach, we, however, often wonder, *When are we going to get there?* There may be wrong turns and detours, injuries along the way, or reluctance to ask for directions. But if you are submissive to her leadership, your mentor will help you make it to the finish line.

Paul was a mentor who challenged his spiritual son, Timothy, up till the very last days of his own life:

> There is going to come a time when people won't listen to the truth, but will go around looking for teachers who will tell them just what they want to hear. They won't listen to what the Bible says but will blithely follow their own misguided ideas. Stand steady, and don't be afraid of suffering

for the Lord. Bring others to Christ. Leave nothing undone that you ought to do.

I say this because I won't be around to help you very much longer. My time has almost run out. Very soon now I will be on my way to heaven.

In heaven a crown is waiting for me which the Lord, the righteous Judge, will give me on that great day of his return. And not just to me, but to all those whose lives show that they are eagerly looking forward to his coming back again.

2 Timothy 4:3-6,8

There is a prize waiting for the faithful, a reward for a life well lived.

The Finish Line

It is so important how we finish. Whether decorating a room, running a race, or living a life, the result is what counts.

As the designer in the family, I am consulted and usually expected to orchestrate some major family events—especially funerals. It is a special honor, however difficult for me, to assist in the last loving touches given to the life of some family member who has gone on to heaven. I coordinated the funeral of my sister Mary Ashley when she died at the age of forty-two. I did the same when my father died five years later.

For forty-three years, Daddy was in the state senate in South Carolina; six years previously he served in the State House of Representatives. He was widely known and beloved for his approachable nature and his wisdom. During his long tenure in office, he gave so much to so many, especially to young men whom he had mentored and championed. After his death, I prayed all day for the Lord to stir some creative idea for bestowing a blessing on those men.

Thinking of the trademarks of Daddy's attire—clip-on tie in the Archibald Cox tradition, suspenders—I decided to select a bow tie from his collection for each of those gentlemen.

On the day of the visitation, thousands of people stopped in to pay their respects at Willbrook, where Daddy had made us promise to bring his body. As he lay in state in the living room, still the grand patriarch of our family, I watched as his constituents, colleagues, and dear friends filed by in an incredible outpouring of love and respect. I was ready for them.

There was Jim, the farmhand who had served Daddy so well for so many years, gazing down into the open casket at his old friend and employer, now cold and still. Without a word, I pressed a bow tie into Jim's hand and saw giant tears form and trickle down his leathery cheeks. There was a prominent doctor who had been able to attend medical school on a scholarship recommended by my father. I stepped forward and placed another tie in his hand.

One by one, the visitors passed by. I spotted those who needed a tangible reminder of their mentor, and repeated the ritual. Healing tears flowed throughout the evening as those grown men wept for the father figure they would sorely miss. It was the most touching tribute I could have given him.

The next day, as I scanned the vast crowd assembled to celebrate Daddy's home going, I was amazed. In that sea of people was the political arena of South Carolina—judges, senators, congressmen. I marveled at how widespread his influence had been. Many of those men were wearing Daddy's bow ties—an unspoken testimony to the love and hope he had given them, a true trophy of grace that far sur-passed Olympic gold.

The day before he died, I spent some time with him in his hospi-tal room, aware that we might not have much time left. I was about to pray for him when he stopped me with an authoritative gesture. "Don't, honey. I won't be coming home. I am tired. You've been a joy to me every day of your life, but it's time to let me go. I'm not afraid to die. I have finished my course."

With that benediction, I could release him. My father had tied everything neatly in a bow for us. He had spoken of the friends and family he would see—grandparents, parents, a daughter—more of them over there now than here—and a big deposit in heaven.

I had left for South Carolina as a daughter, grieving the coming death of my beloved father. I returned to Atlanta as a woman who had put away childish things. With the deposit of one of my greatest treasures in heaven, I would never fear death again.

CHAPTER 18

Inside Heaven's Gates

*And he carried me away in the spirit to a great
and high mountain, and showed me the great city,
the holy Jerusalem, descending out of heaven
from God, having the glory of God....
She had a great and high wall with twelve gates,
and twelve angels at the gates....
And its gates shall not be shut at all.*

REVELATION 21:10,12,25

It was a feast for the eyes!

I had been idly thumbing through the latest issue of an interior design magazine I enjoy when I came upon a room that almost literally transported me to another realm. The scene was the banquet hall of a great castle in Europe.

A long table was set for a very large dinner party. Luxurious European linens of cream damask and sheer silk organza were layered for an opulent yet tasteful look. The fine place settings of china and silver would accommodate every course on the menu, and drinking goblets were of gold and silver and delicate crystal. At either end of the table, two ornate silver epergnes displayed masses of velvety red roses in full bloom, no doubt releasing their fragrance to scent the atmosphere. No walls were visible, merely formless shadows that faded into infinity.

I looked at that table in awe. *This is a vision of paradise! No scene on earth could be this splendid.*

So soon after my father's death, my thoughts turned more and more often to heaven and the deep things of the Lord. I yearned for more of Him. Now that Daddy was with Him, I found myself delving into the Word more passionately and comparing earthly values with heavenly—in my family life, my business and professional life, and with my friends and mentors.

What will it be like, I wondered, *at the Marriage Supper of the Lamb, when God Himself and His Son Jesus and the Holy Spirit, the Creators of the universe, are the Hosts?* The most magnificent settings I have ever seen—the Royal Palace in Madrid, London's Windsor Castle, and Versailles in France—will seem mere residences compared to God's design for His own home and the mansions He has prepared for those who love Him. "In My Father's house are many mansions; if it were not so, I would have told you. I go to prepare a place for you. And if I go and prepare a place for you, I will come again and receive you to Myself; that where I am, there you may be also" (John 14:2,3 NKJV).

A specialist in the interior design of large estates, I *know* mansions. I have shopped the world in pursuit of the finest rugs, the most exquisite antiques, and the greatest paintings, to do justice to the fabulous homes that would showcase them. Yet, even in my wildly creative imagination, I cannot fathom the delights that await us in heaven. I only know what His Word promises, and that He always keeps His promises.

The Vision

John, the beloved disciple, while in deep prayer and praise on the Lord's Day, actually heard the trumpet-like voice of God. As a prisoner on the Isle of Patmos—in the flesh, not in some out-of-body experience—he heard God commanding him to write down everything he would be seeing in the next moments.

The language was not "big" enough or lofty enough to describe what he saw. John was forced to tell us in words that fall far short of the actual vision. When he saw Jesus standing before him—not the Carpenter of Nazareth, but the glorified Son of God—he could only use terms that were *close* to reality, not the reality itself.

> When I turned to see who was speaking...there was one who looked like Jesus who called himself the Son of Man, wearing a long robe circled with a golden band across his chest. His hair was white as wool or snow, and his eyes penetrated like flames of fire. His feet gleamed like burnished bronze, and his voice thundered like the waves against the shore....his face shone like the power of the sun in unclouded brilliance.
>
> Revelation 1:12-16

No wonder John fell at His feet as though dead! (Rev. 1:17.) All he could do was to compare this incredible vision to similar elements in our world. *The heavenly realm is composed of elements so far beyond our comprehension that the design is inexpressible.*

Later, John was caught up in the spirit and witnessed another wonder—an open door into heaven. This time he saw a throne and—oh, the glory of it!—Someone sitting on it! Great bursts of light flashed forth from him as from a glittering diamond or—*wait a minute,* John may have thought—maybe it was more like a shining ruby, and a rainbow glowed like an emerald around his throne. (Rev. 4:2,3.) Can't you feel John's utter amazement and then his frustration in not being able to tell you exactly what he saw that day?

I believe that the earth, the well-crafted copy of the original Paradise, is done in blues and greens, cool colors, while heaven's colors are the rich reds, soft pinks, golds, and metallics. Rather than hiding in the deepest clefts of the rocks and mineral deposits on earth, precious jewels are used as standard building materials in heaven to ornament gates and parapets. Even at best, though, "ye has not seen, nor ear heard, nor have entered into the heart of man [or woman] the things which God has prepared for those who love Him" (1 Cor. 2:9 NKJV). Every little detail will truly boggle the natural mind.

Still, to those who refuse to believe in life after death or feel that God has not given sufficient directions to or about His house, I would suggest reading the entire book of Revelation. While the language may sometimes seem obscure and inexact, those who read the book aloud and those who hear with an open mind and an open heart are both promised a blessing. (Rev. 1:3.) Remember, the word *revelation* means "a revealing,"[1] not a withholding or hiding.

John is not our only mentor in our journey to heaven. We are both warned and encouraged to follow godly people. In writing to the Corinthian Christians, Paul said:

> So don't be proud of following the wise [women] of this world. For God has already given you everything you need. He has given you Paul and Apollos and Peter as your helpers. He has given you the whole world to use, and life and even death are your servants. He has given you all of the present

and all of the future. All are yours, and you belong to Christ, and Christ is God's.

1 Corinthians 3:21-23

We have been given everything we need. Therefore, our destination should be secure. Once we are in heaven, all things will become new.

A New Day

We see in part now, and we will not receive the full vision of heaven until we are there. But we have been promised that in heaven, we will have a chance to start over, to become new creatures. We will each have a new body, a new name, a new song, and a new address.

A New Body

Almost every woman I know would be thrilled with the prospect of a new body, a new and improved model: no cellulite, no wrinkles, no extra pounds! We are assured of just that: a perfect, glorified body, a new design.

Someone will say, "How will the dead be raised up? And with what body do they come?"

The body is sown in corruption, it is raised in incorruption [no sin]. It is sown in dishonor, it is raised in glory [no shame]. It is sown in weakness, it is raised in power [no more arthritis, cancer, or any other terminal illness]. It is sown a natural body, it is raised a spiritual body [no physical limitations].

We shall all be changed.

1 Corinthians 15:35,42-44,51

(For a fuller understanding of the glorified body, see the entire chapter of 1 Corinthians 15.)

We won't be sitting around playing harps in heaven. We will be walking the streets of gold, singing with the angels, praising God, prostrating ourselves before Him, living in mansions, and eating and drinking with Jesus, the Lamb. (See the book of Revelation.)

A New Name

If you are married, your name probably changed when you married your husband. In heaven, God will give you a new name, promised to "[her who overcomes]...a white stone, *[representing victory or special privilege, in this case probably signifying your special ticket to heaven],* and on the stone a new name written which no one knows except him [her] who receives it *[each Christian has a unique relationship to Christ and a unique part to play in God's eternal kingdom]*" (Rev. 2:18 NKJV, italicized section taken from notes in *The Wesley Bible, A Personal Study Bible for Holy Living).*

A New Song

Praise carries us instantly into the presence of the Holy One on this earth, but imagine what it will be like when every voice has achieved perfection and there is complete harmony as we sing to the Lamb: "You were slain, and have redeemed us to God by Your blood out of every tribe and tongue and people and nation, and have made us kings and priests to our God; and we shall reign on the earth" (Rev. 5:9,10 NKJV).

A New Address

A friend once found this description of heaven scribbled on the back of an envelope tucked away in an old Bible:

> Heaven is Company: The cream of humanity's crop.
>
> Heaven is Purity: The state of existence there.
>
> Heaven is Immunity: From all sin and corruption that could enter the gates.
>
> Heaven is Activity: Busy, busy, busy!
>
> Heaven is Identity: We will know each other.
>
> Heaven is Eternity: Beyond the realm of time.
>
> Heaven is Home.

Heaven's Reward System

Not only will we have an invitation to a lavish dinner party, a new body, a new name, a new song, and a new address, but there will be a crown waiting for those who have met the qualifications.

At the Olympics, the coveted award is a gold medal. The competition is intense, with the athletes often winning—or losing—by mere fractions of a second. In the Christian life, the reward is a crown.

The Crown of Righteousness

The true biblical meaning of *righteousness* is far deeper and richer than Webster's weak definition. It has more to do with God's character and covenant than with our good deeds. "Righteousness is the fulfillment of the terms of a covenant between God and humanity or between humans in the full range of human relationships."[2]

When you stand before God, He is not going to judge you on the basis of what you accomplished professionally on this earth or how much money you saved for retirement. He will be more interested in how you answered the call on your life and what you deposited in the lives of others—especially "the least of these" (Matt. 25:45).

This crown comes as a result of dying to self and being resurrected by the Lord in every area of your life. It is given as a prize for withstanding the fires of testing and emerging as pure gold. The crown of righteousness is not about *doing;* it is about *being.*

The Crown of Life

> Happy is the [woman] who doesn't give in and do wrong when [she] is tempted, for afterwards she will get as [her] reward the crown of life that God has promised those who love him.
>
> James 1:12

Satan's mission statement is to tempt, defile, and destroy. The easy path is the walk on the broad way, where the crowd gathers to party. This is the location of all temptation. But once you have resisted—dodged the bullets and snares of the enemy—you are on the path of righteousness, headed for heaven.

While the winner of the Olympic Games of biblical times received a garland of myrtle leaves, even this "crown" was not bestowed unless the athlete obeyed the rules. "Follow the Lord's rules for doing his work, just as an athlete either follows the rules or is disqualified and wins no prize" (2 Tim. 2:5). The only way to receive the crown of life—eternally abundant life with God—is to obey the Lord and His Word, even when you don't understand.

The Crown of Glory

"When the Chief Shepherd appears, you will receive the crown of glory that does not fade away" (1 Peter 5:4 NKJV). "For as you know him better, he will give you, through his great power, everything you need for living a truly good life: he even shares his own glory and his own goodness with us!" (2 Peter 1:3).

The next time we see Jesus, He will call a shareholders' meeting to disperse the dividends of faithful service.

Everything that belongs to the Father will belong to us. "The Spirit Himself bears witness with our spirit that we are children of God, and if children, then heirs—heirs of God and joint heirs with Christ, if indeed we suffer with Him, that we may also be glorified together" (Rom. 8:16,17 NKJV).

Jesus is our Lord and Master, but He is also our elder Brother. By right of kinship, we stand to inherit "all the...rich and wonderful blessings he promised" (2 Peter 1:4).

Equal Opportunity

After the funeral of my friend Lizanne's mother-in-law, the relatives gathered, as relatives always do, to go through her things. Some items would be distributed to other family members, some would be given to charity, and others discarded. When Lizanne opened the dresser drawers in the bedroom, she was astonished to find a peculiar assortment of treasures. Nestled among the nightgowns and lace-trimmed handkerchiefs were a pair of pliers, some batteries, and a couple of fishing lures—apparently all were of equal value to her mother-in-law since they resided side by side in the drawer. In the kitchen was another incongruous pairing—a can of pâté de fois gras next to a pork rind resting on the counter.

It occurred to Lizanne that this was also the way her mother-in-law had lived her life—regarding every *person* alike, despite background or breeding. It seemed to me that her legacy was one of equal opportunity. *How like God,* I thought, *who loves us all just the same and will reward us according to His evaluation of our character.*

Family Reunion

Daddy so loved family gatherings—especially those times when the entire Williams clan came together for the annual Fourth of July picnic. Daddy's daddy was one of nine children born to a wealthy landowner. This great-grandfather believed in family togetherness and arranged to have all of his sons and daughters and their families live nearby. Consequently, our relatives are not scattered all over the globe. I remember many summer outings with aunts and uncles and cousins by the score.

At the reunions there was an incredible amount of food supplied by the good southern cooks in the family. Long banquet-sized tables were mounded with fried chicken, casseroles of every description, Clara's famous deviled eggs and pimiento cheese sandwiches. Several tables were covered with cakes, pies, and other delicious desserts. As children, we found it difficult to wait for the prayer of blessing before our diving in, after which we always ate too much. Then there were games and songs and swimming in the Edisto River until late into the afternoon. These are precious memories.

All of this will pale in the light of heaven's grand family reunion. All of our saved and sanctified forebears, the blood relatives we have never met, will be there. The biblical characters that mentored us indirectly will step out of the pages of the Book to introduce themselves.

The celestial music of the angelic choir will echo throughout the vaulted halls of heaven.

When we've been there 10,000 years, we will sit down for supper at the Marriage Feast of the Lamb. As our gazes sweep the dear faces of those assembled, we'll see our sisters—birth sisters and spiritual sisters—who walked with us for a season.

Alice and Rachel will be reunited with their children.

Brenda will at last realize that not once in her lifetime was there a "holding pattern."

Lizanne will enjoy the fellowship of her mother-in-law.

Patty, Jody, and Linda will see the result of faithful intercession.

Kay and Jean will receive the answers to all the questions of their hearts.

Martha will be carrying on a nonstop conversation with Bertie.

Charlotte will have put down her pen.

Doris will be speechless for the first time in her life.

When we study the "scatter pattern" of Mary's ministry, we will all stand in awe.

Eliza's "children" will have reproduced to multiplied millions.

And just inside heaven's gates, Clara will be one of the first in line to welcome me.

I can still remember the morning my sister died. As my parents and I made arrangements for the funeral, I noticed a peace about Mother that struck me as unusual. She wore a musing sort of look, as if she were entertaining some delightful secret. It seemed inappropriate.

When I asked about it, she replied, "Oh, I was just thinking that Mary Ashley must be having a glorious time in heaven right now. I am sure that my mother and Mother Williams have formed a receiving line and are introducing her to her great-great-great grandparents all the way back."

The thought of those two grande dames observing the social graces in the halls of heaven and presenting my sister to the South Carolina society of the centuries brought a smile to my face for the first time in days. What a comfort to know that our family bloodline—as far back as we have traced our roots—is, we believe, all solidly Christian, all believers of the first magnitude. These many generations of family saints were surely gathering around my sister to welcome her to the inner courts of praise.

Mary Ashley is in heaven today because someone led her there.

Look Around the Table

Look around the table and see who is there because of you. The ripple effect of your obedience will be clearly evident. You have made spiritual deposits in other lives. They, in turn, have mined those rich nuggets, added them to their own giftings, filtered them through their unique experience, and passed them on. Because of your faithfulness, heaven will be fuller and richer. Only then will you know the magnitude of your earthly existence—and why God called you to His kingdom. You will finally get it.

All the loose ends of life will be tied up like one of Daddy's bow ties. The work on earth will have finished. The legacy will have been left behind. There will be no more pages to write. The story will have been told.

The book will have been closed, and a new one will be beginning. It will be the Book of Life, with no more tears, no regrets, no insecurities, no fear, no unanswered questions—and no ending.

Social Graces for Mentorees: Remember Your Manners

Honor your mentor's time. Be prompt. Respect the established beginning and ending times.

Help protect your mentor's privacy and family time. Resist the temptation to be a "midnight caller."

Do not assume that you are her only mentoree.

Acquire the fine art of listening. Do not interrupt when she is imparting some truth to you.

Be thoughtful when you are together. Think of small ways in which you can serve her.

Stay focused and on subject when you are talking.

Invite her to lunch or tea. Find ways to honor her.

Return her generosity by growing in grace and mentoring others.

Pray for your mentor.

When the mentoring season has ended, bless each other with a benediction of thanksgiving. Recognize that you are moving to the next level, and don't feel hurt or rejected when she no longer "has time" for you. God will honor your desire to continue learning and growing and will send another mentor when the time is right.

A Commissioning Prayer

Gracious Father,

Thank You for giving us the gift of mentoring—one life encouraging another.

I pray that each person reading this book will become more aware of Your presence in her life. May she recognize the mentors You will send and receive the blessing they impart.

Enrich our lives with more of You, dear Father. Lead us, Holy Spirit. Teach us and lift us to a higher level.

In Jesus' name—the name that is above all names.

Amen.

Endnotes

Disclaimer
1. Mish, p. 581. "impartation"
2. Ibid., p. 726. "mentoree"

Part 1
1. Guymon, undated.

Chapter 1
1. Pierce.

Chapter 2
1. Butler, p. 703. "inspiration"
2. Ibid, p. 246. "chastening"

Chapter 3
1. Butler, p. 366. "discipline"
2. Ibid.
3. Arndt, p. 362. "thlipsis"

Chapter 4
1. Marshall, pp. 162-170.

Part 2
1. Steen, p. 9.
2. Ibid.

Chapter 6
1. Strongs Greek, p. 876. "apocalypse"

Chapter 7
1. Robertson, p. 101.
2. Ibid.
3. Ibid.
4. Ibid.
5. Mish, p. 742
6. Robertson, p. 102.
7. Meyer, p. 54

Chapter 8
1. Anderson, p. 45.
2. Lewis, p. 163.
3. Heart Songs, p. 251.

Chapter 9
1. Mish, p. 331. "discernment"
2. Finto, p. 154. "sukkoth"

Chapter 10
1. Butler, p. 59.
2. Bynum, pp. 12-18.

Chapter 11
1. Bynum

Chapter 14
1. Flynn, p. 1.

Chapter 15
1. Robertson, p. 103.
2. Hayford, p. 2025.

Chapter 18
1. Mish, p. 1002. "revelation"
2. Butler, p. 1195.

References

Anderson, Keith R. and Randy D. Reese, *Spiritual Mentoring: A Guide for Seeking and Giving Direction.* DownersGrove, IL: InterVarsity Press, 1999.

Arndt, William F. and F. Wilbur Gingrich, eds., *A Greek-English Lexicon of the New Testament and other Christian Literature,* 2nd ed, rev. and augmented. Chicago: University of Chicago Press, 1979.

Butler, Trent C., Ph.D., gen. ed., *Holman's Bible Dictionary.* Nashville, TN: Holman Bible Publishers, 1991.

Bynum, Juanita, "The Ingredients of the Anointing," *Spirit-Led Woman.* February/March 2000.

Finto, Don, *Your People Shall Be My People: How Israel, the Jews and the Christian Church Will Come Together in the Last Days.* Ventura, CA: Regal Books, a Division of Gospel Light, 2001).

Flynn, Leslie B., *What the Church Owes the Jew.* Carlsbad, CA: Magnus Press, 1998.

Guymon, Madame, *Autobiography of Madame Guyon.* Chicago: Moody Press, undated. as quoted in Calvin Miller, *Walking With Saints: Through the Best and Worst Times of Our Lives* (Nashville: Thomas J. Nelson Publishers, 1995.

Hayford, Jack, gen. ed. *Spirit Filled Life Bible* (NKJV). Nashville: Thomas Nelson Publishers, 1991.

Heart Songs: Melodies of Days Gone By. Boston: The Chapple Publishing Company, Ltd., 1909.

Lewis, C. S., *Mere Christianity.* New York: Macmillan Publishing Company, 1943, 1945, 1952.

Marshall, Catherine, *A Man Called Peter: The Story of Peter Marshall.* New York: McGraw-Hill Book Company, Inc., 1951.

Meyer, Joyce, "Who Are We to Pass Judgment?" *SpiritLed Woman.* August/September 2000.

Mish, Frederick C., gen. ed., *Merriam-Webster's Collegiate Dictionary, Tenth Edition.* Springfield, MA: Merriam-Webster, Inc., 1993.

Pierce, Chuck, "Women Transforming the World", *Spirit-Led Woman.* Strang Communications, 2000. www.spiritledwoman.com/wim/pierce.html

Robertson, Pat, *Answers to 200 of Life's Most Probing Questions.* Nashville: Thomas Nelson Publishers, 1981.

Steen, Dorothy Jean Lipham, "Helen Keller Touched My Face and Heart," *Mature Years.* Spring 2000, p. 9.

About the Author

Warm, hospitable, and gracious, Ann Platz epitomizes the qualities that people admire most about the South. Raised with a deep appreciation for the art of beautiful living, she grew up in an ancestral plantation home in Orangeburg, South Carolina. In the mid-'70s Ann moved to Atlanta, Georgia, where she resides with her husband, John. She is the mother of two daughters, Courtney Cloer Norton and Margo Fitzgerald Cloer. Together, she and John have six grandchildren.

Ann has been well-known in the South as an interior designer for over twenty-five years and is a popular and delightful lecturer. Speaking on topics from design and etiquette to the deeper things of the Spirit, Ann warms the heart with her effortless southern elegance and storytelling wit.

She is the author of six other books, including *Social Graces* and *The Pleasure of Your Company.* Her design credentials include a governor's mansion, country clubs, and historic houses, as well as two *Southern Living* idea houses. She and John are members of Mount Paran Church of God. They are active in the Christian community of greater Atlanta.

A Personal Note From the Author

Dear Friends,

Now that we have become acquainted, I want to continue this mentoring relationship God has begun in us. If He has used this book to encourage you or impact your life in some way, I would love to hear from you. I would also be available to speak to your church or women's group, as the Lord leads.

Blessings,
Ann

Please contact me at:

Ann Platz
1266 West Paces Ferry Road, #521
Atlanta, Georgia 30327-2306
(Fax) 404-237-3810

www.annplatz.com

Prayer of Salvation

A born-again, committed relationship with God is the key to a victorious life. Jesus, the Son of God, laid down His life and rose again so that we could spend eternity with Him in heaven and experience His absolute best on earth. The Bible says, "For God so loved the world, that he gave his only begotten Son, that whosoever believeth in him should not perish, but have everlasting life" (John 3:16).

It is the will of God that everyone receive eternal salvation. The way to receive this salvation is to call upon the name of Jesus and confess Him as your Lord. The Bible says, "That if thou shalt confess with thy mouth the Lord Jesus, and shalt believe in thine heart that God hath raised him from the dead, thou shalt be saved. For whosoever shall call upon the name of the Lord shall be saved" (Rom. 10:9,13).

Jesus has given salvation, healing, and countless benefits to all who call upon His name. These benefits can be yours if you receive Him into your heart by praying this prayer:

Heavenly Father, I come to You admitting that I am a sinner. Right now, I choose to turn away from sin, and I ask You to cleanse me of all unrighteousness. I believe that Your Son, Jesus, died on the cross to take away my sins. I also believe that He rose again from the dead so that I may be justified and made righteous through faith in Him. I call upon the name of Jesus Christ to be the Savior and Lord of my life. Jesus, I choose to follow You, and I ask that You fill me with the power of the Holy Spirit. I declare right now that I am a born-again child of God. I am free from sin, and full of the righteousness of God. I am saved in Jesus' name, Amen.

If you have prayed this prayer to receive Jesus Christ as your Savior, or if this book has changed your life, we would like to hear from you. Please write us at:

Harrison House Publishers
P.O. Box 35035
Tulsa, Oklahoma 74153

You can also visit us on the web at
www.harrisonhouse.com

The Harrison House Vision

Proclaiming the truth and the power
Of the Gospel of Jesus Christ
With excellence;

Challenging Christians to
Live victoriously,
Grow spiritually,
Know God intimately.